You Be The Judge

Explorations in Jewish Civil Law

Printed in the United States

The Rohr Jewish Learning Institute
822 Eastern Parkway, Brooklyn, NY 11213

(888) YOUR-JLI/718-221-6900
www.myJLI.com

ר' שמואל שיחי'

בֶּן שְׁמוֹנִים לִגְבוּרוֹת

At eighty [one possesses special] strength
AVOT 5:22

THIS COURSE IS DEDICATED
WITH ADMIRATION AND AFFECTION TO

Mr. Sami Rohr

In tribute to his years of visionary philanthropy
And his towering achievements
In creating a renaissance of Jewish life
For young and old
In communities around the world

May he continue to go from strength to strength
Enjoying health, happiness and prosperity

Bringing joy and blessing to others
As he receives joy and blessing from his family and loved ones

מיט געזונט און מנוחה

You Be The Judge

Jewish Learning Institute

Explorations in Jewish Civil Law

The course **You Be The Judge** has been approved in these states for fulfillment of the requirements for continuing legal education

Alabama
California
Colorado
Georgia
Indiana
Minnesota
Missouri
Nevada
North Carolina
New Mexico
Ohio
Pennsylvania
Rhode Island
South Carolina
Tennessee
Washington

The Rohr Jewish Learning Institute
gratefully acknowledges
the pioneering support of

George and Pamela Rohr

SINCE ITS INCEPTION
the **JLI** has been
a beneficiary of the vision, generosity,
care and concern
of the **Rohr family**

IN THE MERIT OF
the tens of thousands of hours of Torah study
by **JLI** students worldwide
may they be blessed with health,
Yiddishe Nachas from all their loved ones,
and extraordinary success
in all their endeavors

Endorsements for
You Be The Judge Explorations in Jewish Civil Law

"**Many thanks for sharing with me the** exciting curriculum of **"You Be The Judge"** and for the excellent idea of bringing the treasure of Jewish law, a major point of Jewish life and Jewish ethos, to the attention of interested people. The idea is relevant and timely, and I am confident that this venture will enjoy great success.

Israeli Supreme Court Justice Elyakim Rubinstein
Former Attorney General of Israel

"**What one learns from these cases is that** legal adaptation is not just a matter of facing new conditions but thinking harder about what is already implied in old principles. The study of Talmudic law is sobering, challenging, inspiring—and also fun for anyone who enjoys puzzles and discoveries.

Professor Jeremy Rabkin
Department of Government, Cornell University

"**Talmud is concerned with the role of the** human reasoning in the interpretation and application of a "revealed law". Hence the relevance attributed by Talmudic Law to the quality and subtlety of the reasoning in the interclash of opinions. The Law is not an abstraction, but a concretion . . .

Dr. Celso Lafer
Chair of Law Faculty, University of Sao Paulo, Brazil
Former Minister of Foreign Relations of the Federative Republic of Brazil

"**It looks like a remarkably interesting and** important work for layman and scholars alike. This will prove to be a very thoughtful as well as provocative course. I am looking forward to its presentation.

Herbert H. Franks
Past President, Illinois State Bar Association

"**Talmudic law offers students of the law the** perspective of an ancient tradition of jurisprudence. In this course, a brilliant scholar and teacher introduces the subject in a clear and analytical way, using recent decisions of rabbinical courts to illustrate the application of basic principles. There could be no better way of wrestling with the deeper issues that underlie every legal system.

Professor Barry Strauss
Department of History and Classics, Cornell University

"**In reasoned discourse and telling wonderful** stories along the way, Rabbi Eli Silberstein gives us in this book real insight into the way the Talmud applies the law to the actions of individuals and their property.

Professor Roald Hoffman
Nobel Prize Laureate
Department of Chemistry and Chemical Biology, Cornell University

"**The more things change, the more things** stay the same. Would a case decided 1800 years ago in a rabbinical court be decided differently by a modern-day jurist? Is legal reasoning different today in America than in third-century Asia? I endorse and look forward to this fascinating course.

Dennis G. Kainen
Past President, Dade County Bar Association
Member, Florida Bar Board of Governors

"**Art imitates life. The best stories in the** world are true. **"You Be The Judge"** is a great opportunity to learn about Jewish law through the drama and excitement of real people and real cases. I highly recommend it.

Michael Helfant, President and CEO, Marvel Studios

Table of Contents

You Be The Judge

דיני

ממונות בשלשה גזלות וחבלות בשלשה נזק
וחצי נזק תשלומי כפל ותשלומי ארבעה ו
וחמשה בשלשה האונס והמפתה והמוציא
שם רע בשלשה דברי ר' מאיר וחכמים אומרי'
מוציא שם רע בעשרים ושלשה מפני שיש בו
דיני נפשות מכות בשלשה משו' ר' ישמעאל
אמרו בעשרים ושלשה עיבור החדש בשלש'
עיבור השנה בשלש' דברי ר' מאיר רבן שמעון
בן גמליאל אומ' בשלשה מתחילין ובחמשה

You Be the Judge

Lesson 1
Honor Among Thieves

Introduction

Welcome to **"You Be the Judge."** This course addresses the world of Talmudic reasoning and the traditional methods used by Beit Din, the Jewish court of law. Talmud study is the pinnacle of the Jewish intellectual tradition, stimulating much analysis and creative thinking through the ages. We hope this course will succeed in introducing you to the satisfaction and joys of this unique field of study.

Many people think about law as a pragmatic tool for negotiating social change. They see its purpose as increasing economic activity, encouraging social progress, maintaining order, and apportioning resources in a fair and equitable way. The law, first and foremost, must be utilitarian, and a given system is judged by how well it achieves its purposes.

By way of contrast, the Talmudic system centers on a set of legal principles that it upholds with great reverence. The laws transmitted by tradition are viewed as axiomatically true. The aim of most Talmudic discussions is to bring a sense of consistency to the system: identifying the principles that underlie the statutes and using these principles to reliably resolve differences when two statements seem to contradict one another. Talmudic discussion analyzes fine differences between laws, differentiates between similar-sounding concepts, and compares laws that, on the surface, seem totally unrelated.[1]

At times, the Talmudic civil legal system might appear to some as rigid, uncaring, and even unfair. Sometimes the adherence to principle seems to come at the expense of intuitive ethics. But as this course will demonstrate, the adherence to principle over practical intuition reflects the aim and goals of the teachings that our people received at Sinai. In the process of studying Talmudic law, you will be exposed to a whole new way of understanding the meaning of law and justice.

[1] This drive to find consistency in the system inspired much ingenuity and is one of the reasons that Talmud has been such a fruitful training ground for logical analysis and creative problem solving.

Introduction to Ownership
Origins of the Concept of Ownership

Text 1

But when mankind increased in number, craft, and ambition, it became necessary to entertain conceptions of more permanent dominion; and to appropriate to individuals not the immediate use only, but the very substance of the thing to be used. Otherwise innumerable tumults must have arisen, and the good order of the world been continually broken and disturbed, while a variety of persons were striving to get the first occupation of the same thing, or disputing which of them had actually gained it. As human life also grew more and more refined, abundance of conveniences were devised to render it more easy, commodious, and agreeable; as, habitations for shelter and safety, and raiment for warmth and decency. But no man would be at the trouble to provide either, so long as he had only an usufructuary property in them, which was to cease the instant that he quitted possession; if, as soon as he walked out of his tent, or pulled off his garment, the next stranger who came by would have a right to inhabit the one, and to wear the other.

William Blackstone, Commentaries on the Laws of England, vol. 2, ch. 1

William Blackstone (1723-1780), Oxford University professor, author of *Commentaries on the Laws of England* (1765-1769), a four-volume survey of the common law, widely admired for providing an orderly, comprehensive treatment of English law in urbane, lucid prose.

Text 2

יהא קרבנך דומה לקרבנו של אדם הראשון
אדם הראשון לא הקריב לא מן הגזלות ולא מן החמסין שהיה כל ברשותו
אף אתה שהכל ברשותך אל תקריב לא מן הגזילות ולא מן החמסין

Adam [a person] from among you will offer an offering to HaShem (Vayikra/Levitcus 1:2)." Why does it say "Adam"? Just as Adam, the first man, did not bring an offering from that which was stolen, since everything was his, you too, do not bring an offering from that which was stolen.

Midrash, Vayikra Rabah 2:7

Bashert: The Marriage of Souls and Sparks

Text 3

"ארבעים יום קודם יצירת הולד בת קול יוצאת ואומרת:
"בת פלוני לפלוני,בית פלוני לפלוני, שדה פלוני לפלוני"

Forty days before a child's birth, a voice from Heaven declares: This person's daughter will marry that person; this person's house will become that person's; this person's field will become that person's.

Talmud, Sotah 2a

Illicit Contracts

Case Study: The Unscrupulous Assessor

Text 4

Mr. Goldfinger, who owned a house in central Jerusalem, died. His son, who lives in the United States, came to Israel for two days for the unveiling ceremony. Mr. Martin approached the son with a proposal to buy his father's house, with all the furnishings. The son responded to the offer by asking him to have an impartial assessor evaluate the property, and said that he would sell the property if Mr. Martin would be willing to meet the assessed value. Mr. Martin, who was a swindler, contacted a professional assessor of shady character, and promised him a $5,000 kickback, providing he assessed the value of the house and furniture for $60,000. The true value of the house and furnishings was $85,000. After the fraudulent sale had been completed, the assessor asked Mr. Martin for his $5,000. Mr. Martin refused, although he did not deny having promised it, arguing that it was an unethical agreement. The assessor and Mr. Martin came to court. Is Mr. Martin obligated to pay, or not?

You Be the Judge

Do you think Mr. Martin is obligated to pay? Why or why not?

The Hire of a Harlot

Text 5

לֹא תָבִיא אֶתְנַן זוֹנָה וּמְחִיר כֶּלֶב בֵּית ה׳ אֱלֹקֶיךָ לְכָל נֶדֶר
כִּי תוֹעֲבַת ה׳ אֱלֹקֶיךָ גַּם שְׁנֵיהֶם

he hire of a harlot . . . you shall not offer in the Temple of G-d.

Devarim/Deuteronomy 23:19

Text 6

רבא אמר: לעולם כרמי בר חמא
אתנן אסרה תורה ואפילו בא על אמו
ואי תבעה ליה קמן בדינא מי אמרינן ליה קום הב לה אתנן?
אלא אע״ג דכי קא תבעה ליה בדינא אפילו הכי לא אמרינן ליה זיל הב לה
כיון דכי יהיב לה הוי אתנן
הכא נמי אע״ג דלענין תשלומין אי תבע בדינא קמן
לא אמרינן ליה זיל שלים כיון דקא מקני ליה בהכי הויא מכירה

Rava said: "The Torah forbade a harlot's wage even in the case of a son who consorted with his mother. Now, in that case, if the mother sued her son in court for the agreed-upon compensations, would we then say to him, 'Arise, give her the harlot's payment!'? Certainly not! However, although it is clear that if she sued him in court, we would not say to him, 'Go give it to her,' if it happened that he gave it to her in payment, it would be considered a harlot's payment."

Talmud, Bava Kama 70b

Text 7

כיון שצריך לתת לה לצאת ידי שמים חשיב אתנן ולא מתנה
הכי נמי הויא מכירה

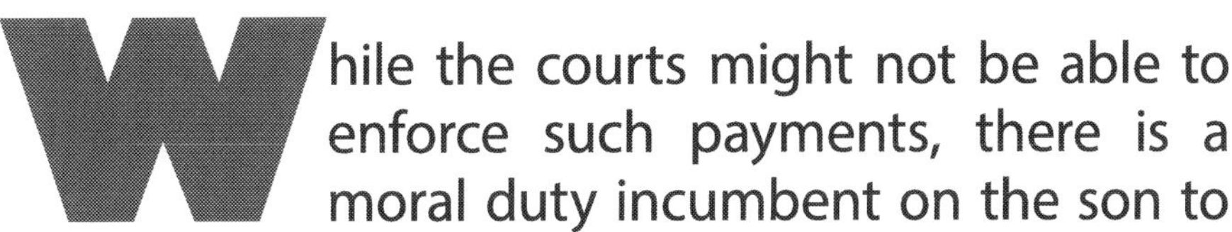

While the courts might not be able to enforce such payments, there is a moral duty incumbent on the son to

Tosafot: Commentaries on the Talmud, by scholars from the 10th-13th century in France and Germany, including Rashi's sons-in-law and grandsons. The Tosafot of *Bava Kama* are ascribed to **R. Yehudah Sirleon,** 1166-1224.

make the agreed-upon payment. Therefore, should the son make the payment, we would see it as a payment, not as a gift.

Tosafot, Bava Kama 70b

Lying Witnesses

Text 8

פעם אחת בקשו בייתוסין להטעות את חכמים
שכרו שני בני אדם בארבע מאות זוז אחד משלנו ואחד משלהם
שלהם העיד עדותו ויצא. שלנו אמרו לו: אמור כיצד ראית את הלבנה?
אמר להם: עולה הייתי במעלה אדומים וראיתיו שהוא
רבוץ בין שני סלעים ראשו דומה לעגל אזניו דומין לגדי קרניו דומות
לצב וזנבו מונחת לו בין ירכותיו והצצתי בו ונרתעתי ונפלתי לאחורי
ואם אין אתם מאמינים לי הרי מאתים זוז צרורין לי בסדיני
אמרו לו: מי הזקיקך לכך?
אמר להם: שמעתי שבקשו בייתוסים להטעות את חכמים
אמרתי: אלך אני ואודיע להם
שמא יבואו בני אדם שאינם מהוגנין ויטעו את חכמים
אמרו לו: מאתים זוז נתונין לך במתנה והשוכרך ימתח על העמוד

One time the Boethusians attempted to deceive the Sages into sanctifying Rosh Chodesh on the wrong day. They hired two people for a total of four hundred zuzim—one of ours and one of their own—to testify falsely that they had seen the new moon. The witness who was one of their own, presented his testimony before the Rabbinic Court and left. When the witness who was one of ours came to give his testimony . . . they [i.e. the Court] said to him, "Tell us how you saw the moon."

He said to them, "I was going up Ma'aleh Adumim and I saw it crouching between two rocks, its head resembling that of a calf, its ears resembling those of a kid, its horns resembling those of a deer, and its tail placed between its legs, and I looked at it and was startled and fell backwards. And if you don't believe me—behold there are two hundred zuzim bundled into my cloak, which I was given to offer this testimony!"

They said to him, "Who involved you in this matter?"

He said to them, "I heard that the Boethusians sought to deceive the Sages, so I said to myself, 'I will go and let them know of my willingness to testify falsely for them, lest unworthy people come and deceive the Sages.'"

Thereupon they [the Sages] said to him, "The two hundred zuzim are given to you as a present, and the one who hired you should be stretched out on the post to be flogged."

Talmud, Rosh Hashanah 22b

Question for Discussion

Based on what we have learned so far, does the witness have the right to keep the two hundred zuzim paid to him for offering false testimony?

Text 9

Rashi: Rabbi Shlomo Ben Yitzchak (1040-1105) of France, considered one of the greatest Jewish scholars of all time. His authoritative commentary on the Talmud is included in all printed versions of the Talmud.

ותהא רשאי לעכבן, ואף על פי שלא השלמת תנאי שלך לשוכרך דיש רשות לבית דין לקנוס ממון ולעשותו הפקר

We give you permission to keep the two hundred zuzim given to you, even though you did not fulfill the terms that they stipulated with you. For the Beit Din has the authority to impose monetary penalties, through their power to declare property ownerless as they see fit, in order to penalize wrongdoers.

Rashi, Talmud Rosh Hashanah 22b

Text 10

Rabbi Moshe Isserles (Rema) (1525-1572) of Poland, renowned halachic authority, wrote *Hamapah,* a commentary on the *Shulchan Aruch,* and *Darkei Mosheh,* a commentary on the *Arba'ah Turim.*

מי שתובעת אשה שנדר לה דבר באתננה והוא כופר חייב לישבע

If a woman charges a man for neglecting the promised payment for sexual favors, and the man denies the charges, he is obligated to swear before the court that the charge is false (just as is the case with any other legally binding contract that is disputed).

Rabbi Moshe Isserles (Rema)
Commentary on Shulchan Aruch, Choshen Mishpat 87:25

Key Points

1. Jewish law is all about consistently upholding principles.

2. From the Jewish perspective, ownership is not a convention but an inherent relationship between the owner and thing owned.

3. Jewish law does not create this relationship through legislation; rather, it responds to the reality.

4. Illicit contracts are valid, despite being illicit.

5. Our possessions are *"bashert,"* i.e., the purpose of our souls is connected to the inherent spiritual potential contained in each object that we own.

Additional Readings

The Legal and the Mystical I

By Rabbi Eli Silberstein

Jewish mysticism is often perceived as ethereal, abstract and beyond the ken of all but a select few. It is often considered to have little relevance to the day-to-day life of an ordinary Jew. Indeed, the laws and commandments found in the Torah and Talmud which form the framework of Jewish living can be understood and followed without any knowledge of the mystical literature. Chasidic philosophy teaches, however, that there is an essential, fundamental interrelationship between all levels of Jewish thought, reflecting the unity of their Divine source. In particular, Chasidism teaches, there is an intimate connection between the mystical and the purely legal dimensions of Jewish thinking. The former is not merely a lens through which we gain a unique perspective on the latter, it is rather an inseparable part of it, without which Jewish law would not be what it is. If the law is the physical body, explains the Zohar, its mystical interpretation is the soul. Through joining body and soul—the legal and the mystical—many difficult-to-understand issues in Jewish law may be clarified.

Mystical Dimensions in Civil Law

It is perhaps not altogether surprising that understanding issues of ritual concern in Jewish law would be enhanced by a mystical approach. Remarkably, however, we also find this dimension in the area of civil law. Although the Torah approach to issues such as acquisitions, loans, torts, and contracts seems on the surface to be in some ways similar to secular systems, it is in reality far more complex.

Consider, for example, ownership—a key concept in the area of civil law. Ownership is central to any discussion of loans, torts and contracts. In secular thought, ownership is normally perceived as no more than a social convention. Society's welfare depends on the implementation of clearly defined boundaries so as to avoid conflict in a world where people compete for the same turf[1]. (An interesting question from this perspective might be whether Adam, while he was alone in the world, owned anything. He had no need to protect objects that he utilized from other potential users.) Jewish mysticism, however, views ownership in an entirely different light. Judaism understands there to be a real metaphysical connection between the proprietor and the property. The Baal Shem Tov explains that every physical object contains a mystical reality, referred to in Jewish mysticism as a divine spark. These sparks are comprised of a G-dly energy which constitutes the essential existence of that object. The purpose of existence, then, is to elevate these sparks from their state of obscurity, and reveal their inherent divinity within the physical; this is accomplished by using the objects in which they are contained to perform divine commandments. Every person is given a share of the physical world—his physical possessions—which are invested of the divine sparks associated with the divine roots of that person's soul[2]. [This may be the key to the Halacha in Beitzah regarding ones belongings in relation to Techumin. This also helps understand the statement by our Sages: "Anyone who steals a "prutah" from another, is as if he takes his soul." See Rambam Hilchot Gezeila Ch. 1 Sefer Likutei Erkim from a Sicha].

Ownership, then, represents the association between the soul and the divine sparks present in the object in question.* Rabbi Yehudah Loew, the Maharal of Prague, sees this preordained relationship between owner and property reflected in the following Talmudic dictum (Kiddushin 59:A): "'If a poor man is trying to take possession of a certain cake, and another comes along and snatches it, he can justifiably be called a wicked man, for he has encroached upon the livelihood of his fellow.' A man who is attempting to buy an item or enter a business transaction, and another comes along and seized the opportunity away from him, the competitor has done an ethical wrong, for the initial buyer can justifiably say, 'why must you ruin my opportunity to profit?' If you wish to do profit you can easily do business elsewhere.'"[3]

The Maharal explains that everything regarding a person's material possessions, from the accumulation of property to the extent of a person's income or the manner in which he achieves that income, is preordained. Negotiations between buyer and seller may be an indication of the preordained bond between buyer and property in question. Thus, depriving the buyer from completing the transaction with the seller is perceived in Jewish law as theft, because it intrudes on the divine establishment of boundaries between territories of ownership.

[This also explains why one may not steal someone's valuables to recover money owed to him (Berochos 5b, Mordechai Bava Kama Perek Hamaniach, Shulchan Aruch Choshen Mishpot 4 (Maharik, Nesivos)). Or to hold someone's deposit in exchange for a debt. (Ketzot Choshen Mishpat 4 in name of Zohar). This also illuminates the Mishnah in Avot: Ten Lo Mi'Shelo She'Ato Ve'Shelcho She'Lo. At first glance it seems difficult to understand how the Mishnah refers to possession as both Shel'cho and She'lo. Furthermore, why does the Mishnah add She'atah, which is not relevant to discussion? See also Yerushalmi Kidushin on the reason why a donation to Hekdesh does not require a formal kinyan but may be realized through speech.]

We find an allusion to this spiritual bond in the words of our Sages: "The righteous value their physical possessions more than their bodies."[4] (The end of this statement is: ". . . because they do not that take which isn't theirs." The connection between the two is somewhat puzzling. But according to the above, there is a very close connection between ownership (upon which the violation of theft is based) and the personal attachment to one's possessions). Chasidic philosophy expands this idea even further. When a physical entity enters our possession, it is changed and uplifted as a result of the interaction between the divine soul of the owner and the spiritual constitution of the object. Indeed, in relating the story of Abraham's purchase of land from Efron, the Hittite, we find that the Torah uses the phrase, "and the land rose to Abraham," from which we may infer that simply by moving from the possession of Efron, the idolater, to the hands of Abraham, the land itself rose in status. [This is also evident in the common Biblical expression regarding the aquisition of property in objective terms, such as: Ve'kom Hasodeh or Ve'yotzo Hasodeh (See parshas Behar).]

It is interesting to note that the word kinyan, which in Hebrew means "possession" or " taking possession," is often used in Biblical Hebrew to describe the inherent relationship between Creator and creation[5]. In the Talmud, it is used to describe a special bond between G-d and particular entities such as Abraham, the Torah, and Israel[6].

The consequence of this intimate bond between owner and property is often reflected in Jewish law, which regards ownership not merely as a legal concept but as a reality that remains unchanged even when the idea of ownership as a utilitarian notion becomes meaningless. Most rabbinic authorities, for instance, believe that the power of ownership is independent of any use or lack thereof which the owner may derive from his property. Jewish law, for example, prohibits the use of a condemned animal for any purpose, from the time it is condemned until it is put to death. And yet, the owner of the condemned animal is still regarded by Jewish law as its rightful owner, making him liable for any damages it may cause between condemnation and death. Likewise, one is guilty of theft if he steals the condemned animal.

Moreover, even when one owns something which by law he is forbidden to own, title of ownership is not legally revoked. This is clearly illustrated by the prohibition to own leavened foodstuffs during Passover. Even so, if a Jew has neglected to sell his leavened foods prior to Passover, he is still regarded as their legal owner[7]. Indeed, it is only possible to violate this prohibition of chometz by owning it. We may infer from all this that not only is the legal concept of ownership not defined by the practical use or benefit derived from the object or property, but it is also not diminished by the legal prohibitions against ownership.

We find a striking illustration of this in the laws of contracts. A contract involving an illegal service, such as one regarding the pay due to a hired hit man, has no legal validity in any secular legal system. This is not surprising: the law is established for the sake of providing a moral framework of conduct; it cannot sanction activities which contradict this principle.[8] In Jewish law, however, this is not the case. The validity of a contract is completely independent of its legality.

Other illustrations of this idea: sale under duress is valid in spite of the illegality of the venture, theft brings certain rights of potential ownership to the thief—i.e. if the object changes etc. (he also enjoys certain rights even before owning it, such as paying according to the value of the time of the theft etc.), finding a lost object without a "Siman," war may be illegal for Bnei Noach if it is not for self-defense purposes and yet the conquest does create a legal validity of ownership for the conquerer (see Le'or Ha'Halocho Ch. 1 in name of Chatam Sofer etc.).

On the other hand, there are situations when theft is permitted and yet does not create ownership, such as stealing under duress to save one's life, which is permitted (and the owner has an obligation to surrender his property to save another's life under "Lo Ta'amod Al Dom Re'acho") but must be reimbursed. (An interesting question would be whether the owner of the property has the right to prevent someone who is in danger from taking his property to save himself. After all, the obligation of "Lo Ta'Amod Al Dom Re'Acho" is a "Lo Ta'aseh" and thus not subject to the rule of "Kofin Oso Ad She'yomar Rotzeh Ani"). In other words, the property is not "Hefker" just because one may steal it or because the owner has a moral and legal obligation to give it up.

Take, for instance, a case where someone engaged in a contract in which he hired two individuals to commit perjury on his behalf. Is he legally obligated to pay the perjurers after they have committed the crime as agreed? When this case was brought to the attention of Rabbi Yakov of Lisa, he ruled that the perjurers are entitled to their fee, in spite of the illegality of the service that the fee is claimed for.[9]

A similar situation was recently brought before a Jerusalem rabbinical court, in which an individual interested in purchasing an apartment agreed to pay the seller an amount set by an impartial assessor. The buyer then went behind the seller's back and made an agreement with the assessor to set the appraised value of the property at a much lower amount than its real worth, in exchange for a five thousand dollar fee. The appraiser fulfilled his side of the agreement, and the sale was executed. When the appraiser demanded his fee, the buyer refused, claiming that such a contract was legally meaningless. They brought their arguments before a rabbinical court. The verdict was unequivocally in favor of the assessor. The contract was enforceable in spite of its illegal nature.[10]

In Jewish law, illegal contracts retain their validity not only when the crime has been committed, but even when the illegal act has yet to take place. Jewish law, for example, forbids two Jews to participate in a loan agreement in which interest is charged; this prohibition applies equally to lender and borrower. Nevertheless, once the loan has been already made under this agreement, the transaction remains valid. In fact, from the perspective of Jewish law, the contractual obligation of the borrower to make his interest payment remains in force; but he is not permitted to fulfill his agreement because of a biblical law prohibiting the taking and charging of interest. So the individual is at once held responsible for his contractual agreement, yet prohibited from fulfilling it by Torah law.[11] While the contract remains valid, it obviously cannot override a Torah prohibition.

This idea is not merely of abstract interest but it has rather tangible legal ramifications. One example of how the laws of usury may be applied in this way concerns the transaction of marriage. If a man gives a woman an object of minimum required value, with the intent (by both parties) of marriage, the two become husband and wife by Jewish law.

Now according to some opinions in the Talmud, the law does not insist upon the transfer of a strictly tangible object to facilitate a marriage contract; the groom may forgive the bride a loan and thus effect the transaction necessary to validate a legal marriage. This raises a question, however, with regards to interest: Would the law find acceptable for the marriage contract, the groom's forgiveness of the interest on a loan to the bride, but not the loan itself? Charging interest on the loan is, we know, prohibited by Torah law. Yet, the interest was agreed upon by both parties.

Many authorities argue that forgiving interest should be no different than forgiving a loan since in principle, the woman owes the creditor interest as agreed upon, but the Torah prohibits her from paying it.

In LeOr HaHalakha, the late Rabbi Zevin takes the issue even further: Imagine two people engaged in an illegal contract, in which the money for the illegal service was paid in advance. The party who paid backs out of the deal before the service has been performed, claiming before the court to have changed his mind because of its illegal nature. The other party claims that since the contract is legally binding, and he is ready to perform the service, he is not obligated to repay the advance.

What is the law in such a case? The court can't tell him to perform the service and keep the money, for the act is against the law. Furthermore, he cannot claim that he is able to perform the service (even though it is technically possible for him to do it), for the force of the law prevents him from doing so! On the other hand, the force of the contract protects the defendant from having to repay the money so long as he is willing to abide by the agreement. In a detailed analysis from talmudic sources, Rabbi Zevin shows conclusively that in such a case the willing party is not obligated to repay his advance. Despite its illegal nature, the contract remains binding on its signatories. The implications of the case point to the strength of a contract; even when it involves forbidden activity, a Torah prohibition is powerless to invalidate it.

It seems problematic that the law should be dictated by two mutually exclusive conditions. For if the law really disapproves of certain agreements, logic dictates that it should invalidate them. Why allow a conflict of legal principles within one system? This is especially bizarre in a religious system whose purpose it is to promote moral behavior. It seems so much more reasonable to invalidate such agreements so as to deter corruption.

This peculiarity, however, is a direct consequence of the unique nature of the Jewish legal system, which acknowledges a mystical reality—such as exists between property and proprietor—and the shift in reality when an agreement is made to transfer property, be it money or even a service. Whereas secular law attempts to construct its own reality by the conditions it imposes on a given situation, Jewish law, by contrast, acknowledges an independent reality, and responds to that reality. Hence, a contract between two people is perceived by Jewish law as a creation of a new metaphysical reality. So although the content of the contract may itself by contrary to Jewish law, this does not in any way invalidate the contract itself.

The ultimate challenge of understanding any given law in the Jewish legal system may be to conceive it in accordance with its mystical counterpart. In an anecdote about Rabbi Chaim of Sanz, a 19th century authority on Jewish law, we are told that he was once observed being deeply absorbed in thought. When asked about his unusual preoccupation, he said that he had just received a letter from Rabbi Menachem Mendel of Lubavitch (author of the Tzemach Tzedek), containing a very complex legal question. To arrive at a resolution that would satisfy Rabbi Menachem Mendel, explained Rabbi Chaim, was a very demanding task, for it required that any legal decision be made in harmony with the mystical teachings concerning the law in question.

Indeed, when seen from the perspective of Jewish mysticism, the commandments are not merely practical tools for enhancing human life, but are themselves the embodiment of a Divine reality.

NOTES

1. John Locke, Second Treatise, Ch. 5; See also Hume's essay on The Origins of Justice and Property; Blackstone, Commentaries on the Laws of England, Vol. II, Ch. 1.

2. See Keter Shem Tov, No. 218; Or Torah, p. 101; Likutei Sichot Vol. 12, p. 118.

* When ownership is transferred, it indicates that the sparks contained in the transferred object require the intervention of more than one soul to be elevated.

3. See Choshen Mishpat 237.

4. For a discussion on the value of material possession over the value of the body, see Likutei Sichot Vol. 15, p. 288.

5. See, for example, Genesis, 14:19, or the Amidah.

6. See end of Pirkei Avot.

7. Rabbi Shneur Zalman of Liadi, Shulkhan Arukh, Hilkhot Pesach, Ch. 435, Kuntres Acharon.

8. See Hendrix v. McKee, 281 Oregon 123 (1978).

9. Netivot Hamishpat No. 9, 1.

10. Responsum Netzach Yisrael No. 17 by Rabbi Yisrael Grossman.

11. Mishne L'Melech, Hilkhot Malve V'love Ch. 8, No. 1; Avnei Miluim, No. 28; Likutei Sichot Vol. 12, p. 119.

Reprinted with permission from *Wellsprings Magazine*, a publication of Lubavitch Youth Organization

You Be The Judge

Lesson 2
Finders Keepers?

Introduction

As you walk down the street, you see a small crowd gathered around a beautiful mansion engulfed in flames. Firefighters are desperately trying to put out the fire, but with little success. The owners of the house are watching in despair and resignation as their home and all its contents are about to go up in smoke. At risk to your life, you dash through the flames, managing to retrieve an expensive original painting from the fire just moments before the house collapses. The owner runs over and embraces you, effusive in his thanks. "That painting," he says, "is a Rembrandt. It is the most expensive item in the house. Thank you for rescuing it for me."

"For you?" you answer in surprise. "I didn't endanger myself in order to return the painting to *you*. You gave up on saving anything from the house. This painting is abandoned property that I recovered, and now it is mine."

Must you return the painting to its owner? Or can you claim it for yourself?

Overview of the Laws of Loss and Recovery of Property

The Obligation to Return Lost Property

Text 1

לֹא תִרְאֶה אֶת שׁוֹר אָחִיךָ אוֹ אֶת שֵׂיוֹ נִדָּחִים
וְהִתְעַלַּמְתָּ מֵהֶם הָשֵׁב תְּשִׁיבֵם לְאָחִיךָ

וְאִם לֹא קָרוֹב אָחִיךָ אֵלֶיךָ וְלֹא יְדַעְתּוֹ
וַאֲסַפְתּוֹ אֶל תּוֹךְ בֵּיתֶךָ וְהָיָה עִמְּךָ עַד דְּרֹשׁ אָחִיךָ אֹתוֹ וַהֲשֵׁבֹתוֹ לוֹ

וְכֵן תַּעֲשֶׂה לַחֲמֹרוֹ וְכֵן תַּעֲשֶׂה לְשִׂמְלָתוֹ
וְכֵן תַּעֲשֶׂה לְכָל אֲבֵדַת אָחִיךָ אֲשֶׁר תֹּאבַד מִמֶּנּוּ וּמְצָאתָהּ

f you see your brother's ox or sheep going astray, you must not ignore them. You must return them to your brother.

If your brother is not near you, or if you do not know who the owner is, you must bring the animal home and keep it until your brother identifies it, whereupon you must return it to him.

You must do the same with a donkey, an article of clothing, or anything else that your brother loses and finds. You must not ignore it.

Devarim/Deuteronomy 22: 1-3

Text 2

אף השמלה היתה בכלל כל אלו ולמה יצאת?
להקיש אליה לומר לך: מה שמלה מיוחדת שיש בה סימנין ויש לה תובעין
אף כל דבר שיש בו סימנין ויש לו תובעים חייב להכריז

In this passage the Torah says that a finder must return "every lost thing of your brother's," but it also singles out for special mention a lost ox, ass, lamb, and garment . . .] Since the garment is obviously merely a particular example that is already included in the Torah's general command to return all lost property, why was it singled out and mentioned explicitly? . . . Lost garments were singled out to illustrate a point, to make us compare garments with other lost objects. [The Torah is saying to us:] Only objects that are similar to garments must be returned. A garment is special in that there are identifying marks on it and, as a result, it has claimants. It is a man-made object in which its owner has made some investment, and thus he will not give up hope of recovering it. So too must everything that has identifying marks on it and has claimants be announced. But lost objects that are not marked or not likely to be claimed need not be returned, because their owner will have given up hope of recovering them.

Talmud, Bava Metsia 27a

Questions for Discussion

1. According to the Talmud, in what way do garments differ from the other examples mentioned in the text?

2. By the inclusion of the example of garments in the text, what do we learn about the limits upon the obligation to return lost objects?

Text 3

מניין לאבידה ששטפה נהר שהיא מותרת?
שנאמר "כן תעשה לכל אבדת אחיך אשר תאבד ממנו ומצאתה"
מי שאבודה הימנו ומצויה אצל כל אדם
יצתה זו שאבודה הימנו ואינה מצויה אצל כל אדם

From where in the Torah do we know that a lost object of any kind, even one containing an identifying mark, that was swept away by a river is always permitted to be kept by the finder, and need not be returned to its original owner? As it says: "So shall you do with every lost thing of your brother's, which is lost from *him,* and which you have found." From the presence of the seemingly superfluous word *"from him,"* the rabbis drew the following conclusion: Only that which is lost *"from him"*—i.e. as far as its owner alone is concerned—but is available to everyone else, must be returned. By inference, this excludes an item which was swept away by the river—which is not only lost to its owner, but is not available to anyone else either—since the river is likely to carry it away altogether. Accordingly, the Torah declares such an object to be ownerless, and it need not be returned, even if the original ownership is not in dispute.

Talmud, Bava Metsia 27a

Text 4a

המציל מהארי והדוב וזוטו של ים ושלוליתו של נהר הרי אלו שלו

If someone salvages property from a lion, a bear, the rising sea, or an overflowing river, it belongs to him.

Rabbi Yosef Caro, Shulchan Aruch, Choshen Mishpat 289:7

Rabbi Yosef Caro of Safed (1488-1575), author of the *Shulchan Aruch,* "the Set Table," a compilation of Halachah recognized as authoritative by all Jewish communities. Born in Spain, he fled the Inquisition at the age of four with his family.

Text 4b

שיירא שהיתה הולכת במדבר ועמד עליה גייס וטרפה
אם אינם יכולים להציל מידם
ועמד אחד מהם והציל הציל לעצמו

A group of people was traveling through a desert and a [large] group of bandits robbed them of their belongings. Then, [if] one of the travelers [risked his life and] managed to save an object from the hands of the looters; he may keep it . . . as the owner surely despaired of recovering it.

Rabbi Yosef Caro, Shulchan Aruch, Choshen Mishpat 181:1

Rabbi Moshe Isserles (Rema) (1525-1572) of Poland, renowned halachic authority, wrote *Hamapah,* a commentary on the *Shulchan Aruch,* and *Darkei Mosheh,* a commentary on the *Arba'ah Turim.*

Text 4c

owever, it is good and just to return it.

Rabbi Moshe Isserles (Rema)
Commentary on Shulchan Aruch, Chosen Mishpat 259:7

Text 5

Hebrew books [which were stolen] are always regarded as being [in a state] before [the onset of] despair. For it is not common for an owner of Hebrew books to despair of recovering the stolen books. The looter will inevitably sell those books to a Jew, who will then return them to its owner.

Rabbi Moshe Isserles (Rema)
Commentary on Shulchan Aruch, Chosen Mishpat 181:1,
based on Tosafot, Bava Kama 114b

Applications
Books Pillaged during the Holocaust

Case Study: The Case of the Looted Books

Text 6

I was asked the following question: During World War II, the Slovak [Nazi puppet] government looted the property of the Jewish population. The current government of Slovakia now has thousands of Hebrew books and sacred manuscripts, which they are ready to sell. Is it permitted for a Jew to buy those books and keep them as his own?

Rabbi Yaakov Breish, Chelkat Yaakov, vo1. 1, no. 136

Rabbi Yaakov Breish (1895-1976), respected halachist, born in Galicia, died in Zurich. Author of *Chelkat Yaakov,* a collection of responsa.

You Be the Judge

May a Jew buy these looted books for the purpose of keeping them as his own?

Text 7

However, it seems that in our case the buyer would not have a legal obligation to return the books to their owners . . . The reason which Tosafot gives for the exception applying to stolen books is that the owners expect the looters to sell the books to Jews [as no one else would be interested in those books]. However, in the case of the Holocaust, we know how the original owners of these books where exiled from their homes, with nothing on their bodies, and there was no justice available for these poor victims. Furthermore, we know what was done to Jewish books in other lands of bloodshed [during the Nazi control of Europe], where they burned the Jewish books publicly.

Rabbi Yaakov Breish, Chelkat Yaakov, vol. 1, p. 136

Text 8

Despair of recovering stolen property does not normally occur with regard to stolen sacred books because the only way the thief may profit from such stolen items is by selling them to a Jew. Hence, the victim has no reason to despair of the return of such property. But, this consideration did not apply during WWII because the Nazis were intent upon annihilating the entire Jewish people and it therefore did not enter the mind of any person that the books would again come into the hands of Jews, since from the day of the creation of the universe there never was a terrible edict such as this—to annihilate, to slay, and to destroy all Israel. In such a state, if they already despaired of their lives, did they not most certainly [despair] of their property? To whom would it occur to think thoughts of his house or fortune while under the nails of the angel of death, the impure foul oppressor, in the death camps and in the ghettos?

Rabbi Isaac Liebes, Teshuvot Beit Avi, vol. 1 no. 157, cited and translated by Rabbi David J. Bleich, ed. Contemporary Halakhic Problems, vol. 3, p. 355

Rabbi Isaac Liebes, respected contemporary halachist, author of *Teshuvot Beit Avi,* a collection of responsa about the Holocaust.

Text 9

The Germans often used to take entire Jewish libraries and preserve them, as they did with our library that is now in its entirety in Prague. Hope never fled from our heart [during the Holocaust] that this evil power would vanish like smoke . . .

Rabbi Yechiel Yaakov Weinberg, Seridei Eish, vol. 1, no. 147

Rabbi Yechiel Yaakov Weinberg (1885-1966), very influential Talmudic scholar. He studied at the "traditionalist" Slobodka and Mir yeshivahs, but served as rector at the Berlin Rabbinical Seminary during the 1930s, where he became associated with the approach of Rabbi Samson Raphael Hirsch. He settled in Switzerland after WWII. His legal rulings, many on problems of modern life, are collected in several volumes under the title, *Seridei Eish,* i.e., "Remnants of Fire."

Acquisition via Conquest (optional section)

Text 10

עמון ומואב טהרו בסיחון

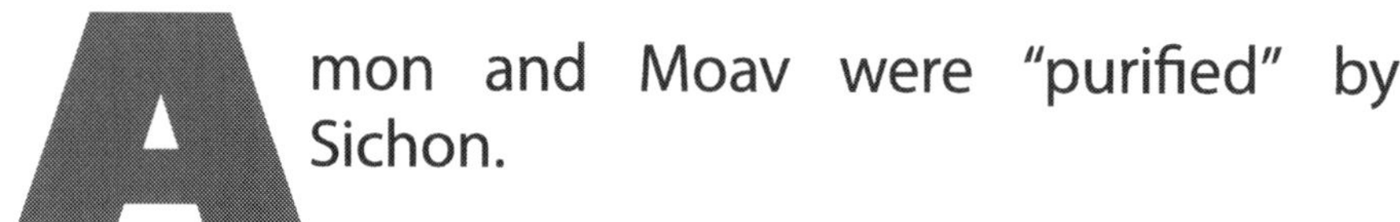

Amon and Moav were "purified" by Sichon.

Talmud, Gitin 38a

You Be the Judge

Might Nazi governments be granted ownership of Jewish possessions under the principle of conquest?

Text 11

In our case the principle of conquest does not apply, as the Nazis attacked the Jews who were living securely on their land, under their sovereignty. The goods that they stole from the Jews could not be considered spoils of war. It should be categorized as plain robbery . . .

Piskei Din Shel Batei Hadin Harabaniyim, vol. 1, p. 169

The Legal and the Mystical
Justice and Ethics

Text 12

Our Sages teach that one is not required to return a lost object to its rightful owner, if the owner has despaired of ever recovering it. This seems unfair to many people's sensibilities. For how could someone take possession of someone else's property?

However, the Torah's legal system is not a system of logical ethics. In a logical ethical system, it would have made sense to return a lost object even if the owner despaired of recovering it, as logical ethical systems concern themselves with the maintenance of social order, and for the sake of social order it seems more plausible to grant the lost object to the original owner. Conversely, if someone found gold or silver vessels [which have an identifying mark] and the finder made an attempt to publicize it once or twice, yet no one came forward to claim it in more then a year or two, [logical ethics] would dictate that the finder should then keep it for himself, as it appears unlikely that the owner would ever come back to claim it.

But in Torah law this would not be the case. For even if one publicized the lost property numerous times, the object might never be claimed by the finder. It must be stored [in a safe communal location] "until Elijah arrives."

The law of Torah is based on principle. It does not follow an intuitive sense of reasoning. It follows a wisdom which is free of pragmatic intuitions. Strict principles of ownership dictate that when an object has been removed from the owner's consciousness (i.e. by giving up on finding it), the object is no longer in the domain of ownership of the original owner, as property is not a piece of the proprietor's body which he cannot separate from; it is his possession which can be removed from his domain of ownership . . .

And if someone will argue: True, strict principles of ownership dictate that despair of an object should result in the automatic suspension of ownership, but from an ethical standpoint, shouldn't one return the object anyway so that the owner does not suffer a loss? The answer is that the Sages in the Talmud indeed said that ethically one should return the object, although not as legal requirement but as a kindness to the owner. The Rabbis derived from the Torah itself a mandate for one to act beyond the strict letter of the law and to do kindness toward others. In this way the Torah is a perfect system where it maintains laws which are consistent with principle and truth, while encouraging acts of kindness and ethics.

Rabbi Yehudah Loew of Prague, Be'er HaGolah, pp. 31-32

Rabbi Yehudah Loew of Prague (1525-1609), "the Maharal," thinker and mystic. Author of *Gevurat HaShem*. Thousands visit his resting place in the old Jewish cemetery of Prague every year.

Key Points

1. As soon as one despairs of reclaiming a lost object, it becomes ownerless.

2. Jewish legalists assess under what circumstances there is no hope for an object's return and under what circumstances hope remains.

3. The laws of lost objects once again illustrate how principle is more important than a pragmatic solution that appears fair.

4. According to Jewish mysticism, strict adherence to law does not create justice, but allows the divine order to unfold.

Additional Readings

The Return of Lost Property According to Jewish & Common Law: A Comparison

By Michael J. Broyde[1] & Michael Hecht

I. Introduction

In every legal system a gap exists between the law as it is actually enforced by the courts and the ethical categorical imperative.[2] Although it was rejected by Justice Holmes in his "bad man rule,"[3] a strong claim can be made that the measure of an enlightened and advanced legal system and society is its success in bridging this gap. Within a religious legal system[4] which rejects the clear separation of law and ethics, the severity of this problem is ameliorated. As illustrated by Jewish law, even such a system's purely civil law must be influenced by ethical duties to a far greater degree than in secular legal systems.[5]

This article compares the legal rules and jurisprudence of the American common law and Jewish law in the area of finding and returning lost or abandoned property, illustrating the interplay between the purely legal and ethical components of the respective legal systems. Surprisingly enough, the differences between the two systems are not usually significant; they follow the same basic legal principles, and typically lead to the same results.[6] There is, however, one major exception: Jewish law imposes a duty to rescue the lost property of one's neighbor, while the common law does not require that one initiate the process by retrieving the article. Thus according to Jewish law, when one happens to stumble across lost property, one must intervene to retrieve it; according to the common law one need not. Second, Jewish law imposes ethical duties as part of its legal mandate, a practice the common law does not follow.[7]

This article approaches the issues raised in returning lost property in the order they are encountered as property is lost or found. The first two sections discuss the issue of defining "lost property;" the next four sections discuss the obligations of the finder; the subsequent two sections discuss the legal relationship between the finder and the original owner; and the last section discuss miscellaneous issues related to lost property.

II. When is Property "Lost"?

Jewish law recognizes that property may become ownerless by one of two means: (1) abandonment, which is an express renunciation by the former owner of his ownership; or (2) express or implied "forsaking hope" of reclaiming an object to which one has legal title, but not possession by the owner of that item. Abandonment is effective only for property in one's own possession at the time of abandonment. By contrast, forsaking hope is applicable to both lost and stolen property; it is a relinquishment of the right to have the property returned. It results from external, involuntary circumstances which have placed the property beyond the possession of the owner, and the owner's realization that he is unlikely to ever recover his property. These juridical concepts in Jewish law find nearly perfect analogy in the common law doctrines of relinquishment and abandonment. For example, after abandonment in Jewish law and abandonment in common law, the finder of lost property can properly exercise dominion over the object, thereby vesting title and absolute ownership in himself.

While this legal rule is quite clear in both legal systems, its applications are underdeveloped in common law compared to Jewish law. The critical question is: what factual circumstances warrant a finder to conclude that abandonment by the initial owner has occurred? A noted writer on the common law of personal property indicates that the common law is hazy and undeveloped on this question. "No cases have been discovered dealing with the question of the circumstances that would justify a finder in assuming dominion over lost goods on the assumption that the owner had abandoned them, or could not be discovered."[8]

Jewish law, on the other hand, provides a detailed set of rules which regulate when abandonment has occurred or may be presumed. The finder may gain title to the lost property if abandonment has expressly occurred, or if it may be reasonably presumed. One illustration of express abandonment is presented by the Talmudic scholar, Rabbi Zvid. "The general principle in regard to a loss [of property] is if (the loser) has said 'Woe! I have sustained a monetary loss,' he has abandoned his object."[9] No prior communication of the declaration of abandonment to the finder is necessary.

The circumstances in Jewish law in which abandonment may be presumed has generated far more discussion. The Mishnah,[10] discussing which type of property cannot be presumed to be abandoned,[11] explains that the finder's duty of the public proclamation applies if two conditions are satisfied: the object must have (1) claimants; and (2) identifying marks or signs which would allow the original owner to identify the object as his. An owner of a lost article, the Mishnah posits, cannot be expected to have abandoned hope for its return if he has means of identifying the object, and he knows that the law requires that one return objects to its rightful owner. However, once he is aware of the loss, the owner can be expected to abandon hope of recovery if the lost item has no unique identifying marks which would allow him to reclaim his object.[12]

Jewish law added one further element to determine whether one can presume abandonment of a lost object or is obligated to seek out the owner and return the find. This is the concept of *yeush shelo medat*, literally abandonment without knowledge, which is the subject of an involved and famous Talmudic dispute.[13] The concept is applied to lost property not identifiable by unique marks—situations where Jewish law would normally assume abandonment. If the finder takes possession of lost property prior to the owner's awareness of his loss, the latter's *subsequent abandonment* is ineffective and the property must be returned to the owner once his identity is satisfactorily established. In his analysis of this rule, Rabbi Isaac Herzog, states that through the application of this principle, "the scope of abandonment is considerably reduced."[14] Indeed, he comments, "The reader may well wonder under what conditions abandonment is effective."[15] Although there undoubtedly is some truth to this assertion, it unnecessarily overestimates the practical consequences entailed by the application of this principle. The Talmud provides detailed guidelines which aid the finder to reasonably conclude that the owner became aware of the loss shortly after its occurrence, or in any event, before it was found, permitting the finder to properly assume title. For example, the loss of money is presumed to be discovered virtually immediately by the loser since "a person usually touches his wallet at frequent intervals."[16] Likewise, the Talmud places in this category particularly precious items, and those which are heavy, since people quickly notice the loss of such items.[17] So too, an object which has been lost for a long time (even if it has a unique identifying mark) is presumed to be abandoned, since Jewish law assumes that people eventually discover losses of property.[18]

However, the legal principle of *unintentional abandonment*—that in order for abandonment to be effective it must precede the finder's taking possession—presents analytic and jurisprudential problems within Jewish law. The Talmud appears to indicate that the finder took the article *in violation of the law*, without right, since an unknowing owner is not capable of abandonment which would entitle the finder to claim ownership, and any subsequent abandonment is not given retroactive effect for the benefit of the finder. This seems to be the explanation of the Tosafists.[19] Yet, this argument contains an inherent difficulty, for it is appropriate to apply the improper conduct concept only to a case of theft and not to one of lost property.[20] Nahmanides, obviously aware of the difficulty implicit in this approach, offers an entirely different rationale[21] to explain the ineffectiveness of unknowing abandonment, based on the premise that abandonment is possible only if the object is not in fact within the possession of the one abandoning the object. He argues that since the finder took possession of the lost article prior to abandonment and thereby became a bailee of the owner, the owner's subsequent abandoning hope of recovery is not effective since one cannot abandon hope of recovering property which is legally considered within his own possession, and the possession of the bailee is considered that of his bailor.[22] Whichever approach one takes, it is clear that abandonment is only effective prior to finding the object.[23] Such a result stands in contrast to the law in New York State, which, in its recodification of the lost property laws, rejects all of the common law (and Jewish law) formalism and defines "lost property" as follows:

Lost or mislaid property. Abandoned property, waifs and treasure trove, and other property which is found, shall be presumed to be lost property and such presumption shall be conclusive unless it is established in an action or proceeding commenced within six months after the date of the finding that the property is not lost property.[24]

In New York, property is lost when the owner does not know where it is.

III. When is Property "Mislaid" Rather than "Lost"?

Jewish law recognizes a fundamental distinction between lost property and mislaid property.

While Jewish law compels a person to affirmatively act when he encounters lost property,[25] no such obligation is present for mislaid property. One who encounters mislaid property not only need not pick it up, indeed one is prohibited from picking up the property, whether to find its original owner or to claim it as lost.[26] The rationale for this is obvious: if the property is placed in a particular place (that is relatively secure), the easiest way to ensure that the object is returned to its owner is to do nothing: the owner will return to retrieve his possession.[27] If one picks up the mislaid property in violation of Jewish law, one must attempt to return the property to its owner; even if the owner is never found, the finder never takes valid title, since the initial act of picking up the object was not lawful.[28]

The identical distinction is found in the common law. As one well known treatise on personal property states: To intentionally place an article down and then go away, forgetting it, has often been held not a losing of it; thus the discoverer of the article is not a "finder" and does not have a finder's rights.[29]

According to common law, one who places an item down deliberately has created some form of a bailment with the one on whose property the item is left.[30] The "finder" of the item is not the finder according to common law, but must leave it as a bailment with the person on whose property it was found, since the one who mislaid the property is most likely to remember where the item was placed, and return to that spot to retrieve his item.

On a practical level, both Jewish and common law found it difficult to distinguish between mislaid and lost property in "hard" cases. Jewish law resolved these issues by creating a presumption in favor of mislaid property. If doubt exists whether the article was deposited or lost, the finder should not assume possession.[31] Rabbi Moses Isserless[32] adds a number of additional factors. He distinguishes three situations: (1) The object is located in a reasonably safe location.

Here, the law is, as stated above, that the finder should not touch the object whether identifiable by identifying marks or not, as long as reasonable doubt exists that it was intentionally deposited rather than dropped;

(2) The article is located in a place where its safety is doubtful.

In this case, if doubt exists whether it is deposited or dropped, the finder is obligated to take and proclaim the find if identifying marks are present. If there are no identifying marks, the object should not be touched, as moving it would decrease the likelihood on locating the original owner.

(3) The object is situated in a place where it definitely is not safe, e.g., a public highway.

Here, if no identifying marks are present, the finder may take possession and title of the object even though reasonable doubt exists that it was deposited there, provided it is an object whose loss would be already noted by its owner, thus allowing for the presumption of prior abandonment. If identifying marks are present, the finder must seek out the owner and return his lost property to him.

Common law, like Jewish law, looked to the place where the object was found as the crucial factor in determining whether an item was lost or misplaced. Thus: if the owner laid the property down in a public place, in a place of business as in a private compartment of a safe deposit company or other place . . . it is not lost, but mislaid, property. But where the articles are accidentally dropped in any public place, public thoroughfare or street they are lost in the legal sense.[33]

New York State, on the other hand, abolished the distinction between lost and misplaced property for the purposes of the laws of lost property. It does not matter how or why property is without an owner; all such property is lost.[34]

IV. When Does One Become a "Finder"?

The crucial distinction between Jewish and common law arises in determining when one becomes a finder. Common law is generally reluctant to impose any affirmative duties on a stranger to protect either the life or property of another; hence, no involvement or obligation is imposed on one who merely sees the lost property of another. It is entirely at the option of the finder to decide whether he will or will not take possession of the object.[35] According to common law, once the finder chooses to volunteer and take possession, only then will the common law impose affirmative duties of any kind. Thus, according to common law one who sees the lost property of another, just like one who sees another drowning, is under no obligation to rescue the property (or the person).[36] New York, accepting the common law rule, states that the "finder" means the person who first takes possession of lost property.[37]

Of course, according to common law and New York statute, one may not take the property as one's own merely because one is not obligated to return it. "Found or discovered property may be the subject of larceny if the finder at the time the article is found . . . knows or has the means of ascertaining the owner, or believes the owner can be found but nevertheless intends at that time to appropriate the article for his own use."[38] Thus, according to the common law, one can walk away from lost property and not get involved; however, if one gets involved, one must follow the rules.

By contrast, Jewish law, a system which imposes duties even in the absence of special relationships, requires that one who sees lost property must involve himself in that property and assist in its return. The origin of this lost property doctrine is in the Bible. Three verses in the Bible[39] provide the basis for the obligation to involve oneself in the lost property of another:

1] When you see your brother's ox or sheep going astray do not ignore them; you must return them to him.

2] But if your brother does not live near you, or you do not know who he is, you should bring it home to your house, and it shall remain with you until your brother claims it; then you shall give it back to him.

3] You should do the same with his donkey; you should do the same with his garment; so you should do with anything that your brother loses and you find; you have no right to withdraw [from returning it].

Jewish law accepts, based on these verses, that there is a legal imperative to intervene and return the lost property of another. Furthermore, this is in harmony with Jewish law generally, which imposes a duty upon all members of the community to intervene to aid another member of the community.[40]

The exact parameters of the obligation to assist in property return are of some dispute within Jewish law. Most authorities[41] are of the opinion that one who sees lost property and then declines to pick it up has transgressed both the negative prohibition of "you have no right to withdraw [from returning it]" and the positive commandment of "you shall give it back to him."[42] A number of authorities adopt a different understanding, which is closer (albeit by no means identical) to the common law rule. These authorities rule that if one is aware that visible property is lost, but never takes physical possession of the lost object, he is only guilty of transgressing the negative prohibition of "you have no right to withdraw [from returning it];" the positive commandment of "you shall give it back to him" does not apply unless the finder takes actual possession and does not return the object.[43]

However, according to both opinions, there is a clear legal obligation to retrieve the lost property of another. Jewish law allows no option to one who comes upon such property as to whether he should become involved.[44] Nevertheless, virtually all authorities maintain that one who violates this obligation and deliberately passes over the lost object of another and the item is subsequently never returned incurs no legally enforceable duty of compensation to the person whose object was lost, although it is right and proper to do so.[45] Essentially, the obligation to stop and involve oneself in the lost property of another is an ethical duty whose violation is without financial penalty. Of course, one who picks up a lost, unabandoned item with the intent of taking actual possession of the item without returning it to its original owner has committed an act of theft for which compensation is required. In addition, such a person has violated both the positive and the two negative commandments to return lost property.[46]

Yet, it is interesting to note that according to both Jewish and common law one who picks up lost property intending to return it, and upon examining it determines that there are no marks on it which will enable the finder to identify the owner is, is not guilty of theft, even if by due diligence the owner could have been found (and the owner is still looking for the object). According to Jewish law, such conduct typically violates the obligation to return lost property (but is not theft) and according to the common law such conduct is conversion, but not theft.[47]

The religious duty of aiding a stranger with whom one has no prior (legal) relationship has become the cornerstone of the Jewish law. This is but one example of many where the Jewish law imposes an ethical obligation to come to the aid of a stranger to protect either his physical or spiritual well-being or his property.[48]

V. Duties of the Bailee-Finder

The basic duty of the finder according to both Jewish and common law is to restore the lost object to its owner. When the loser's identity is known or can be simply determined, (for example when the object contains his name) the Talmud, based on a scriptural[49] inference, rules that the return may be made either to the owner personally or to his possessory domain. When one returns an object to the owner's domain, it is not even necessary to inform the owner that his object has been returned.[50] So too, according to the common law, "a finder is under a duty to ascertain the owner of the article found" and to return it.[51]

What are the legal duties in a situation where the object's owner is not known, but the object contains clear markings that would allow one to return the object should the owner realize who has found it? Here, Jewish law imposed a heavier burden. Jewish law imposes on the bailee-finder a duty of public proclamation designed to alert the original owner that his property has been found. Much Talmudic and post-Talmudic discussion revolves about the most effective manner in which the public notice of the find can be conveyed to the owner (without also conveying too much information so as to allow a non-owner to claim the property).[52] Jewish law does not, however, require that the finder suffer any actual financial loss (or even loss of profit) while seeking to return the object.[53] Jewish law requires that one expend free time, but not one's money, in the search for the object's owner.

Common law did not extend the obligation to find the owner even to the expending of one's free time. "While a finder is under a duty to ascertain the owner of the article found, there is no obligation to expend time or money in searching for him if the finder does not have any means of knowing who the owner is."[54] The finder only has to engage in a minimal searching that involves the expenditure of only very small amounts of time or effort.[55] New York law has shifted the burden of searching from the person who finds the object to the police. The law requires: [A]ny person who finds lost property of the value of twenty dollars or more or comes into possession of property of the value of twenty dollars or more with knowledge that it is lost property or found property shall, within ten days after the finding or acquisition of possession thereof, either return it to the owner or report such finding or acquisition of possession and deposit such property in a police station or police headquarters . . .[56]

Indeed, one who keeps the property for more than ten days—even with the intent to search for and find the true owner—is "guilty of a misdemeanor and upon conviction thereof shall be punished by a fine of not more than one hundred dollars or imprisonment not exceeding six months or both."[57] It is the police who are charged with the duty to find the "true" owner in New York; the finder has no legal obligations to search.[58]

VI. What Happens to Lost Property Whose Owner is Never Found?

According to both Jewish and common law, upon taking possession of a lost article, the finder becomes a bailee and remains one until the owner recovers the object. If a reasonable period for publicizing the find has passed, and no one has come forward with a claim, the finder remains a bailee. For how long does the finder remain a bailee? According to Jewish law, he remains a bailee until the owner claims the object, or as Maimonides put it, "until Elijah comes" [and reveals the owner's identity].[59] Common law states that after reasonable efforts to find the true owner, "the finder of lost goods does not gain title thereto as against the [true] owner . . . The finder of lost goods is a bailee of them for the true owner with certain rights and obligations . . . As to all others, however the finder's rights are tantamount to ownership, giving him the right to possess and hold the found goods."[60] *Thus, neither in Jewish nor common law can one acquire title to lost property through one's inability—even after good faith efforts—to find the original owner.*[61]

However, both Jewish and common law accept that although one does not acquire title to the object, one is not completely precluded from using it. There are two schools of thought on this topic within Jewish law. Most authorities, following the rule of Rabbi Shabtai Meir HaCohen, state that in situations where Jewish law precludes the finder from taking title and the law states that the "the object should reside until Elijah comes," that phrase is properly understood to mean "the object should reside *in the finder's pocket* until Elijah comes"—while the user has no ownership rights to the object, it is his to use and derive benefit.[62] Should the finder break it or wear it out, he owes the owner the value of the object, if the owner comes forward and claims it.[63] This seems to be the approach of most decisors.[64] Other Jewish law authorities disagree, and rule that in situations where the owner does not come forward, the object resides in peace, without anyone authorized to use it for his own benefit.[65] According to neither of these schools of thought may the possessor (who is not the true owner) legally transmit valid title to another.

As explained above, the common law held that "[t]he mere fact of finding is not sufficient to vest in the finder any right to title to the thing found;"[66] furthermore, "the finder is only the apparent general owner of the thing found, under an uncertain or contingent title which may be defeated by the discovery of the true owner."[67] According to the common law rule, the finder, after reasonable efforts to locate the true owner, becomes the possessory owner, with a right to usage.[68] However, as in Jewish Law, the possessory owner may not transfer valid title to another.[69] New York State, on the other hand, has rejected this legal analysis and ruled that "[t]he title to lost property . . . shall vest in the finder."[70] New York law essentially directs that in situations where the true owner cannot be found after a reasonable period of time and compliance with the details of the statute,[71] *title* vests in the finder.

In sum, both Jewish and common law (but not New York law) adopted the same rule: one who picks up a lost article prior to abandonment never takes complete title to the object. The original owner always has superior title to as compared to the finder.

VII. What Type of Bailment is Created Between the Finder and the Owner?

Jewish law recognizes essentially three categories of bailment, each with varying degrees of responsibility: 1) The gratuitous bailee, who is liable only for negligence; 2) The bailee-for-hire, who is also liable for theft or loss; and 3) The borrower, who is virtually an insurer, and liable for almost all mishaps which may befall the article.[72]

The Talmud cites two opinions concerning the category of bailment created when one finds lost property. "A bailee of lost property: Rabbah ruled that he is a gratuitous bailee; Rabbi Joseph maintained that he was a bailee-for-hire."[73] It is unclear which of these two opinions Jewish law accepts as normative. Many early authorities including Maimonides and Joseph Karo, the author of *Shulhan Arukh*,[74] rule in accordance with the opinion of Rabbi Joseph and therefore hold the finder responsible not only for negligence, but also theft or loss not attributable to negligence.[75] Many other authorities, including Rabbi Moses Isserless accept the opinion of Rabbah, and rule that the finder only has the status of a gratuitous bailee, and is liable only for his negligence.[76] This dispute remains unresolved in Jewish law,[77] and whoever is the possessor is given the benefit of the doubt, and has applied to him the legal standard that would be most beneficial.[78] In a situation where there is no possessor most authorities rule that the law is in accordance with those authorities who state that the person is a bailee-for-hire.[79]

The opinion classifying the finder as a bailee-for-hire requires explanation. Why should a person who is involuntarily returning lost property assume the status of a paid bailee? Rabbi Joseph[80] renders his opinion based on an overtly religious doctrine of *esek bemitzva*, the rule that while one is engaged in the actual performance of a legally compulsory religious duty, one is excused from other legal obligations, including financial obligations. Thus, Rabbi Joseph recounts that if perchance while the bailee was attending to the lost article for the owner's benefit[81]—a legally compulsory duty—a poor man came for a donation, one would be excused from giving him charity, and such charity is otherwise mandatory.[82] His involvement in attending to a lost object exempts the bailee from attending to the poor man (which would otherwise be obligatory), thereby allowing the returner of lost property to derive a clear financial benefit from his action; such a benefit qualifies as a payment. This financial benefit, according to Rabbi Joseph, is sufficient, without more, to classify the finder of lost property as a bailee-for-hire, since he can derive financial benefit from his bailment.[83] This outcome is unlikely, however, and that is why some authorities accept the opinion of Rabbah and rule that since the financial gain is sufficiently remote, a finder should better be classified as a gratuitous bailee.

The precise dispute as to the status of the finder occurs in the common law. As one authority states: The finder of lost property who takes possession of it assumes the duties of a *bailee without compensation* although some authorities hold the finder to be a *bailee for hire*.[84]

However, in common law, the majority opinion is that the finder is a gratuitous bailee, with only a minority of authorities accepting the bailee for hire rule.[85] Both opinions can be logically understood within the framework of the common law. One need only be a gratuitous bailee, since one's actions are completely voluntary; according to common law, one need not even pick up the lost object. To burden the volunteer by imposing upon him obligations of a paid bailee would only further discourage one from rescuing lost property. On the other hand, there is a reasonable chance that the finder will derive a monetary benefit from his actions, since if the true owner does not come forward, the finder stands to gain use of the property rent free. Thus one could classify him as a bailee for hire, since he is seeking to rescue the property with the hope of using it.[86]

VIII. Is the Finder Entitled to Compensation?

According to both Jewish law[87] and the common law[88] the finder of lost property is not entitled to a reward, unless one is explicitly offered.[89] However, each legal system enables the finder to recover reasonable out-of-pocket expenses incurred in the successful recovery and preservation of the goods.[90] According to the common law, the finder is entitled to recover any loss caused by his involvement in recovery and return of the object, as long as the expenses are reasonable.[91] Jewish law ruled that such a level of compensation is too high. A statement of the Mishnah is the basis for an involved discussion among the early commentaries concerning the remuneration that the finder may claim if he is a worker and his involvement with the lost article has caused him to abandon his own work.[92] The Mishnah, states: "[i]f his lost time is worth a *sela* [a talmudic coin], he cannot demand a *sela*, but is paid as a laborer."[93] The Talmud explains that he is paid as an "unemployed laborer" in his particular occupation.[94] Two different measures of compensation are advanced to explain what an "unemployed laborer" is paid:

1] Many authorities, including Maimonides[95] and Karo,[96] explain that the amount an unemployed laborer is paid is arrived at by estimating how much *less than full pay* an individual in the finder's profession would accept *to remain idle rather than to work.*

2] Other authorities ask how much *less than his full pay* would this worker accept to avoid his regular work and instead *spend his time returning lost objects.*[97]

By definition, both awards are less than the full value of lost time to which he would be entitled under the common law. In other words, Jewish law agrees with the common law and grants a full recovery for out of pocket expenses. For loss of time, which is not an out of pocket expense, but rather the loss of an anticipated profit, Jewish law refuses to concur with the common law and does not allow the full measure of recovery; since the finder is obligated by Jewish law—divine commandment—it is unfair to grant him full pay, when he is additionally receiving divine reward for doing a mitzvah.[98] However, in a situation where the worker's employment is so competitive (or so easy) that a worker would only take time off for full pay, he is entitled to full pay.[99]

IX. How Does the Finder Identify the Owner?

According to both Jewish and common law, there is an obligation to return the item to the original owner, and to make an effort to find that original owner.[100] However, how does a finder determine if the person who is claiming the article actually is the true owner, and not a person who lost a similar item and mistakenly thinks this item is his, or a thief trying to claim an item which is not really his? This dilemma is particularly problematic, since both Jewish and common law make a finder strictly liable if he returns the item to the wrong person and the true owner subsequently claims the item.[101] Jewish law addressed this issue at great length, while the common law left this as a matter of fact to be determined in each individual case, (although the legal principles used by both systems are similar).

According to Jewish law one must return lost property to a person who provides witnesses that the item is his, or recounts unique characteristics of the item so as to make it highly likely that the item is his.[102] Whether the requirement that the finder return the object to one who furnishes indicia of true ownership is of biblical origin or a later enactment of the Rabbis is the subject of an extensive Talmudic discussion.[103] The Talmud offers a practical reason to explain the opinion which views these marks (*simanim*) as a pragmatic Rabbinic institution, a possibility that a thief might be able to furnish adequate *simanim* is clearly outweighed by the possibility that the rightful owner would be foreclosed from pursuing his property for lack of witnesses.[104] Early authorities attempt to resolve this dispute by distinguishing among three different kinds of signs or symbols.[105] First, striking, distinguishing characteristics ordinarily not found in such an object are efficacious to establish ownership, a universally accepted fact and on a biblical level.[106] The classic Talmudic example is the identification of a lost document by furnishing the information that a hole may be found next to a particular letter. It is nearly universally accepted that such marking are efficacious to establish facts even *on a biblical level*. The Talmudic controversy as to whether such marks are a Rabbinic institution or of biblical origin bears on the second level, uncommon marks. This category embraces such factors as exact size, weight, number, and location of find.[107] These types of marks are common to many items, but it is unlikely that anyone but the owner would know them for a particular object. The third category, minimal marks, comprises those identifying characteristics which are not sufficiently unique to be accorded reliability, e.g., a general description of size or color such as large, small, red, etc.[108]

Jewish law generally accepts that one returns lost property to an honorable person if that person presents marks of the middle category—uncommon marks.[109] The Sages added an additional condition to this rule: one should not return an object to an unknown person until that person presents some proof that he is an honorable person, and not a thief.[110]

The common law presented a similar type of legal rule, albeit without the detailed developments found in Jewish law. When the true owner discovered his object, and the finder refused to return the object, the owner would follow the civil procedure of that particular locale for reclaiming one's property in the possession of another. In common law of old, typically that was either trover or replevin, and if the finder claimed title, conversion.[111] Unlike Jewish law, common law and New York law treated the return of lost property no differently than any other civil case between two claimants, with one party claiming ownership of an item in the possession of another. There are hardly any cases which discuss *how* one goes about proving that one is the original owner of lost property; that presumably was the province of a jury or judge determination. For example, a recent New York case involved a true owner suing a finder of airplane tools who had mistakenly given the tools to a third party who claimed to be the owner (but wasn't as determined by the court). The court ruled that:

At common law, a finder was entitled to the use, possession, and enjoyment of any property he had found as against the whole world, except for the true owner. It also followed, at common law, that a finder was not liable, civilly or criminally, for keeping the property he had found against all false claims of ownership, or even against claims of ownership which the finder reasonably believed to be false. Yet, at common law, if a possessor of goods, such as a finder, delivered property to a third person whom he reasonably believed to be the true owner—but was mistaken as to that fact—he became liable to claims by the true owner, notwithstanding his delivery of the found property to a third person by honest mistake.[112]

In the current New York statute, there is no discussion of the remedy available to an owner whose item is returned to the wrong person by the police. Certainly the finder is not liable. There simply is no case law on the liability of the police for improperly returning items to someone other than the owner.

Thus, while Jewish law has a much more legally detailed system, the basic rules used by Jewish and common law remain the same in this area.

X. Salvage from Destruction: An Exception to the Rules?

A unique application of the rules of abandonment and relinquishment occurs in both Jewish and common law: the case of salvage from destruction.[113] The Talmud recounts that one who rescues property facing destruction unpreventable by its owners or agents, acquires title to the property, even if the original owner is present, asserts ownership and denies that he constructively abandoned the property.[114] Some authorities, most notably Maimonides, accept that this rule is an application of the general rules of abandonment, and that when the owner really can prove that he never relinquished the object, it remains his.[115] However, most authorities reject this interpretation, and rule that once an object is about to be destroyed, and its owners are helpless to prevent this destruction, abandonment is legally imposed, and the item is ownerless as a matter of law.[116] In these cases, an express negation of intent to abandon by the owner would be of no avail. As the Talmud comments, "It is as if one protested against his house collapsing or against his ship sinking in the sea."[117] The presumption of abandonment in these instances is so strong that no negation will be given effect, either because the law decides that the negation is not consistent with the owner's true state of mind[118] or, even if consistent, the law refuses to recognize unrealistic intent so contrary to normal behavior.[119]

Common law too had an exception to its general rules of lost property in the case of items facing destruction rather than loss. Common law authorized two distinctly different types of payment in that context. The first was called "salvage;" in the context of maritime law, one who saved another's vessel or property from destruction[120] was entitled to a reward that would be determined by the court. Unlike all other circumstances, this payment was not necessarily related to the value of the services rendered, but was based on a number of factors, including the social utility of the work done, its risks, and many other factors unrelated to the normal rules used to compensate one for unrequested work done.[121] This rule, however, was limited to situations where salvage occurred at sea; in all other circumstances, one who saves another's property from potential destruction intending to be paid for that service is entitled to payment based on quasi-contract, "based on the assumed [common law] obligation of compensation by one who has been enriched by the non-officious act of another."[122] Thus, one who saw another's house burning, and rescued goods from the house was entitled to payment based on how much a person would have paid for those services at that time. This is considerably more than compensation for lost wages generally given by the common law to one who returns lost property in lieu of hourly work.

New York law, it would appear, continued the common law tradition that no reward would be given in all cases of land-based salvage and (at least implicitly) rejected the notion of compensation for "finding" lost objects threatened by destruction. However, New York's lost property law explicitly excludes from its regulation maritime salvage[123] and New York continues to grant rewards for maritime salvage.[124]

XI. Above and Beyond the Obligation of the Law

Jewish law adds one additional "rule." In any case where the finder has the legal right to assume title to the lost property, Jewish law[125] provides that one who wishes to follow the good and righteous path should act beyond the requirements of the law,[126] and return all identifiable lost property even though the circumstances would dictate an irrebuttable presumption of abandonment. Indeed, several authorities[127] are of the opinion that the option of acting above the requirements of the law is not left to the individual as a matter of personal choice, but is imposed, by force if necessary, as a matter of duty by a Jewish court. This opinion is based on the well-known Talmudic statement: "Jerusalem was destroyed only . . . because they based their judgments strictly on the law of the Torah and did not act beyond the letter of the law."[128]

Obviously, the common law, as well as New York law, each a system of purely secular law and not a religious legal system, imposes no such extra-legal duties.

XII. Conclusion

This comparison of the underlying principles used by Jewish and common law in the field of returning lost or misplaced property provokes a number of fascinating insights: As is commonly observed, Jewish law imposes duties in situations where the common law does not; so too, Jewish law is willing to use the law to advance ethical values not normally considered as "law" by the common law. Jewish law is quicker to infuse morality and religion into even the most technical areas of the law.

What is startling is that a comparison of Jewish law with the common law in the area of returning lost property reveals that there are many areas of near identity in the legal rules: in fact, the overlap is nearly astonishing. Jewish law and common law provide very similar or identical answers to eleven of the thirteen questions posed, or an 84% overlap. As shown in Chart A, Jewish law and New York law provide very similar or identical answers to only two of the thirteen basic questions posed or an overlap of 16%. Common law and New York law provide very similar or identical answers to four of the thirteen questions posed, for an overlap of 32%.[129]

Chart A . Jewish, Common and New York Law in the Area of Lost Property			
Legal system Issue	**Jewish Law**	**Common Law**	**New York Law**
When does one become a finder?	Seeing	Possession	Possession
Is there a distinction between lost and mislaid property?	Yes	Yes	No
Is the finder a bailee?	Yes	Yes	No
What type of bailee is the finder?	Majority: for hire Minority: gratuitous	Majority: gratuitous Minority: for hire	Not applicable
Can the finder ever acquire title unless owner abandoned or relinquishes?	No	No	Yes
Does the finder have title superior to all but owner?	Yes	Yes	Not superior to police
Is finder entitled to a reward from loser?	No	No	No
Is the finder entitled to expense reimbursement?	Yes	Yes	Yes
Is the finder obligated to compensate true owner if item returned to person other than true owner?	Yes	Yes	No if police err
Is there a salvage exception?	Yes	Yes	Partially
Who is responsible for finding true owner?	Finder	Finder	Police
Are there any extra-legal duties	Yes	No	No
What happens to lost property whose owner never appears, but which was not abandoned?	Finder can use it but never gains title	Finder can use it but never gains title	Finder gains title

Jewish law and common law provide very similar or identical answers to eleven of the thirteen questions posed, or an 84% overlap. Jewish law and New York law provide very similar or identical answers to two of the thirteen questions posed or an overlap of 16%. Common law and New York law provide very similar or identical answers to four of the thirteen questions posed, for an overlap of 32%. All three legal system provide very similar or identical answers to each other in two of the thirteen questions posed, for an overlap of 16%.

Notes

1. Michael Broyde is a Senior Lecturer in Law at Emory University School of Law and Director of the Law and Religion Program's Project on Law, Religion and the Family; Michael Hecht is the Associate Dean of Yeshiva College and a Professor in the Department of Political Science at Yeshiva College. The research assistance of Paul Malek of Emory University and Tzvi Shiloni of Yeshiva University.

One area of lost property law is not discussed; Jewish law's ruling concerning the role of *makom* (place) and the obligation to return the lost property of a Gentile are omitted from this article and will be addressed in a forthcoming article by these authors entitled "The Gentile and Returning Lost Property According to Jewish Law: A Theory of Reciprocity," forthcoming in the Jewish Law Annual.

2. See *e.g.* Isaac Herzog, "Moral Rights and Duties in Jewish Law" in Volume I of The Main Institutions of Jewish Law (London, 1936), pp. 381-386 for an excellent general analysis of moral claims in Jewish law as compared with those in English common law.

A brief historical review will familiarize the new reader of Jewish law with its history and development. The Pentateuch (the five books of Moses, the *Torah*) is the historical touchstone document of Jewish law and, according to Jewish legal theory, was revealed to Moses at Mount Sinai. The Prophets and Writings, the other two parts of the Hebrew Bible, were written over the next 700 years, and the Jewish canon was closed around the year 200 before the common era ("B.C.E."). From the close of the canon until 250 of the common era ("C. E.") is referred to as the era of the *Tannaim*, the redactors of Jewish law, whose period closed with the editing of the *Mishnah* by Rabbi Judah the Patriarch. The next five centuries was the epoch in which the two Talmuds (Babylonian and Jerusalem) were written and edited by scholars called *Amoraim* ("those who recount" Jewish law) and *Savoraim* ("those who ponder" Jewish law). The Babylonian Talmud is of greater legal significance than the Jerusalem Talmud and is a more complete work.

The post-Talmudic era is conventionally divided into three periods: (1) the era of the *Geonim*, scholars who lived in Babylonia until the mid-eleventh century; (2) the era of the *Rishonim* (the early authorities), who lived in North Africa, Spain, Franco-Germany, and Egypt until the end of the fourteenth century; and (3) the period of the *Aharonim* (the latter authorities), which encompasses all scholars of Jewish law from the fifteenth century up to this era. From the period of the mid-fourteenth century until the early seventeenth century, Jewish law underwent a period of codification, which lead to the acceptance of the law code format of Rabbi Joseph Karo, called the *Shulhan Arukh*, as the basis for modern Jewish law. The *Shulhan Arukh* (and the *Arba'ah Turim* of Rabbi Jacob ben Asher, which preceded it) divided Jewish law into four separate areas: *Orah Hayyim* is devoted to daily, Sabbath, and holiday laws; *Even Ha-Ezer* addresses family law, including financial aspects; *Hoshen Mishpat* codifies financial law; and *Yoreh Deah* contains dietary laws as well as other miscellaneous legal matter. Many significant scholars—themselves as important as Rabbi Karo in status and authority — wrote annotations to his code which made the work and its surrounding comments the modern touchstone of Jewish law. The most recent complete edition of the *Shulhan Arukh* (Vilna, 1896) contains no less than 113 separate commentaries on the text of Rabbi Karo. In addition, hundreds of other volumes of commentary have been published as self-standing works, a process that continues to this very day. Besides the law codes and commentaries, for the last 1200 years, Jewish law authorities have addressed specific questions of Jewish law in written *responsa* (in question and answer form). Collections of such *responsa* have been published, providing guidance not only to later authorities and to the community at large. Finally, since the establishment of the State of Israel in 1948, the rabbinical courts of Israel have published their written opinions deciding cases on a variety of matters.

3. Justice Holmes subscribed to the view, extremely popular in its day, that the law should only attempt to provide guidance for acceptable "legal" rather than proper conduct; thus Justice Holmes was of the opinion that: If you want to know the law and nothing else, you must look at it as a bad man, who cares only for the material consequences which such knowledge enables him to predict, and not as a good one, who finds his reasons for conduct, whether inside the law or outside of it, in the vaguer sanctions of conscience.

Oliver Wendell Holmes, *The Path of the Law*, 10 Harv. L. Rev. 457, 459 (1897).

4. A system in which law is but one component of a religious system. For two recent Hebrew works that are nearly restatements of the Jewish law and ethics in the area of lost property, see Ezra Bassri, Dinnai Mammonut, Volume 3:pages 42-82 (Jerusalem, 1990, 2d ed.) and Jacob Blau, Pithei Hoshen Volume 1 ("Laws of Loans and Lost Property") (Jerusalem 1983). In addition, a long review article on this topic can be found in Encyclopedia Talmudic 11:54-100 "Returning Lost Property."

5. This area of the law was chosen for a number of other reasons also. First, it is an area of the law far distant from any apparent religious significance, thus making it an excellent paradigm for comparing the civil law of a religious system with the civil law of a secular system. Second, from the perspective of the common law, the

field of lost property is devoid of constitutional or federal interests, thus allowing the common law to develop in its historical manner.

6. In Chart A, at the end of this article, we summarize these distinctions in tabular form. In order to demonstrate that this overlap is not an inevitable result that any legal system would have reached, this article—and the chart—also include the legal results that would be reached in New York State which in 1958 recodified its laws of lost property and moved them away from the common (and Jewish) law rules.

7. Neither author is well trained in legal history thus will not claim that the common law was in fact influenced by Jewish law in its analysis of this area, rather than merely co-evolving in the same way as a matter of coincidence. However, given the significant overlap in the substantive legal rules used (and the fact that these rules are not the only one's possible, as demonstrated by New York's complete, but different, statutory structure), it would not come as a surprise if such an influence were shown, nor would this be the first time such an influence has been shown; see Shapiro, *Shetar's Effect on English Law-A Law of the Jews became the Law of the Land*, 71 Georgetown Law Journal 1179 (1982) and Bruz, *The Privilege Against Self-incrimination in Anglo-American law: The Influence of Jewish Law*, in Jewish Law and Current Legal Problems, ed. Nahum Rakover, (1984) at page 161.

8. Ray Brown, The Law of Personal Property, 3rd ed. (CBC, 1975), p.32 n.4 [Hereinafter, Brown, Personal Property]; Common law operates under the general assumption that property is lost and abandonment has not yet occurred; see Paset v. Old Orchard Bank & Trust Co., 19 Ill.Dec. 389, 62 Ill.App.3d 534, 378 N.E.2d 1264 (Ill. App 1978); Martha's Vineyard Scuba Headquarters, Inc v. Unidentified, Wrecked and Abandoned Steam Vessel, 833 F.2d 1059 (1st Cir. 1987).

A claim could be made that the absence of development in this area of common law results from common law being driven by the case method. One suspects that frequently people simply take possession of lost property without a clear legal determination of their right to do so. Common law only allowed for development of this law in the rare circumstance where all of the following six events occurred: (1) Property was lost in a context where abandonment might, but need not, have occurred; (2) the property was found by another; (3) the original owner discovered who found his property; (4) the finder refused to return the object; (5) the original owner sued to recover the object; (6) there was a legal dispute (rather than a factual dispute) that resulted in an appellate decision. Jewish law, since it is driven by legal scholarship, developed definitions of abandonment even in the absence of a case.

9. Bava Meziah 23a; Moses Maimonides, Mishnah Torah, *Theft and Abandonment* 14:3.

10. Bava Meziah 27a.

11. See infra section III for a further discussion of this issue.

12. Joseph Karo, Shulhan Arukh, Hoshen Mishpat 262:6; Pithei Hoshen, supra note 3, at 2:5-7.

13. Bava Meziah 21b-22b.

14. Main Institutions of Jewish Law, supra note 1, at 1:307.

15. Ibid.

16. Bava Meziah 21b; Shulhan Arukh, Hoshen Mishpat 262:3.

17. Bava Meziah 21b; Shulhan Arukh, Hoshen Mishpat 262:3.

18. After a reasonably long time, it is presumed that they abandon hope ever having their property returned, even if it is clearly marked. Shulhan Arukh, Hoshen Mishpat 262:5. For a discussion of what happens to such property, see supra section VI.

19. See Jacob Lorberbaum, Netivot Hamishpat 259, citing Tosafot, Bava Meziah 26a s.v. v'nezel. See also Tosafot, Bava Kama 66a where Tosaphot, carrying this point to its logical conclusion, states that one who picks up an object before abandonment occurs, no longer holds the item as a bailment for the original owner after

abandonment, but rather takes ownership of the item and owes the value of the item to the original owner as a debt. Tosafot's assertion becomes crucial for determining what happens to these items after abandonment; see also section IV for a further discussion of this issue.

20. See Bava Kama 66a where the "in violation" rule is applied to theft and specifically indicates that it does not apply to lost property. That discussion can be understood to apply only if abandonment preceded the finding. Rabbi Yom Tov Ashbealli (Ritva), quoted by Shita Mekubezet on Bava Meziah 26a, compounds the problem by pointing out that the finder is under an affirmative obligation to take lost property into his possession and attempt to find the owner. He, therefore, understands that the Talmudic statement "possession acquired in a prohibited manner" merely indicates that no abandonment has been made, thus entitling the finder to acquire title.

21. Nahmanides, Milhamot Hashem on Alfasi, Bava Meziah 26a. Whether Nahmanides' or Tosafot's rationale is deemed correct is of critical importance in determining what happens to these items; see also section IV.

22. Emanuel Rackman has cited unknowing abandonment as an illustration of Jewish law's attempt to improve the ethical values of the Jewish people, since clearly this principle of law could hardly ever become the subject of litigation. Since the rule is applied to property not identifiable by unique marks, the practicality of the situation virtually insures that the true owner will never recover what he once possessed. Yet the finder is precluded from asserting ownership over the object, and is subject to the same duties, to be discussed below, that are applied to the finder who can reasonably expect that he will eventually be required to deliver the property back to the original owner. As Rackman concludes, "Through such a rule the mores of the people with regard to lost property were improved for the rule was an essential part of the education of Jews throughout the ages." Emanuel Rackman, Legislating with Regard ti Racial and Religious Discrimination," Masmid: Yearbook of Yeshiva College 1948 at pages 49-50.

23. Nahmanides' rationale would be accepted by the common law as correct. According to the common law, abandonment cannot be valid unless one both abandons claim to an item and also abandons actual physical ownership of the item; one who announces intent to abandon an item without actually relinquishing control has not abandoned the property as a matter of law according to common law; see Abandoned, Lost and Unclaimed Property, 1 American Jurisprudence 2d 15 [hereinafter Abandoned, 1 Am. Jur 2d.]

24. Laws of New York, supra note 5, at 251

25. See supra, section IV.

26. Shulhan Arukh, Hoshen Mishpat 260:9-10 and 262:7.

27. It seems clear that even Jewish law, which requires that one take possession of lost property and return it to its owner, does not require that one guard deliberately placed properties to prevent their theft; Pithei Hoshen, supra note 3, at 4:(n.3).

28. Moses Isserless (Rama), commenting on Shulhan Arukh, Hoshen Mishpat 260:9. This is in accordance with the general Jewish law rule that abandonment does not grant the possessor valid title if the possessor himself acquired the item improperly.

29. Ray Brown, Personal Property, supra note 7, at 29. The statement in the second edition of Personal Property, written more closely conforming to the common law rule, states: To intentionally place an article down and then go away, forgetting it, is not in the eyes of the law a losing of it, nor is the subsequent discoverer of such an article the finder thereof. Ray Brown, Personal Property, (2nd Edition, Chicago, 1955) at II:24.

30. See e.g., Kincaid v. Eaton 98 Mass 139 (1867); McAvoy v. Medina, 11 Allen 548 (Mass. 1866). What exactly happens to these items will be discussed supra in section IV.

31. For example, if an animal is found roaming in the fields during the day, or an object buried in the sand, or a garment or spade is found by the side of a field fence, the finder should conclude that the owner will return and retrieve their items; see Shulhan Arukh, Hoshen Mishpat 261:1-2.

32. Shulhan Arukh, Hoshen Mishpat 260:10.

33. Abandoned Property, 1 Am. Jur 2d., supra note 22, at 3.

34. See supra, text accompanying note 23.

35. Ray Brown, Personal Property, supra note 7, at p.30. Cf. Murgoo v. Cogswell, 15. D. Smith 359. It, of course, is sometimes an extra-legal obligation to become involved in returning lost property; see Frank Childs, Principles of the Law of Personal Property (Callaghan, 1914) p.443 ("A person seeing lost property is not under any legal obligation to take it into his possession, however great this moral obligation to do so may be...").

36. This is also consistent with general common law rule which requires a special legal relationship to be present before the common law imposes a duty. This special legal relationship can be contractual, such as employer-employee, biological, i.e. parent-child, or involuntary such as a tort-feasor's relationship with the victim.

37. Laws of New York, supra note 5, at 251. Thus in a case where two boys discovered an envelope containing $12,300 in cash, and sought the assistance from a 15-year-old girl who — with the two boys — took the money to her house, all three are finders for the purpose of the law. Edmonds v. Ronella, 73 Misc.2d 598, 342 N.Y.S.2d 408 (1973).

38. Childs, Personal Property, supra note 34, at 337 (451-452).

39. Deuteronomy 22:1-3.

40. The approach of Jewish law to aiding members of the community is based on the verse "[d]o not stand [by idly] and let your brother's blood be spilled." Leviticus 19:16. Based on this, and other textual imperatives, Jewish law generally imposes a duty to intervene so as to protect others from injury.

41. See, e.g., Rabbi Solomon Yitzhaki (Rashi), commenting on Bava Meziah 30a; Yosef Habib, Nimukei Yosef, Bava Meziah 30a; Moses Maimonides, Mishnah Torah, Theft and Abandonment 11:1; David Halevy, Turai Zahav (Taz), Shulhan Arukh, Hoshen Mishpat 259.

42. For a lengthy discussion of this, see Pithei Hoshen, supra note 3, at 1:1 (and notes accompanying section). Jewish law draws jurisprudential distinctions between positive and negative commandments which are beyond the scope of this article. For an explanation of these differences, see Menachem Elon, Hamishpat Haivri (Third Edition, Jerusalem, 1988) pages 185-199.

43. See Yosef Habib, Nimukei Yosef, commenting on Alfasi, Bava Metzia 30a, and Joshua Falk-Cohen, Sefer Meirat Einayim, Shulhan Arukh, Hoshen Mishpat 259:1. This clause is based on the statement in Bava Metzia 26b that if the finder waits until the owner abandons hope of recovery by expressing abandonment and then takes the article, he has transgressed only the "you have no right to withdraw [from returning it];" See Nahmanides, Commentary on Bava Meztia 30a and Falk-Cohen, cited above. However, most authorities disagree. They distinguish Bava Metzia 26b on the grounds that one cannot be said to have negated the command "you shall give it back to him" without some positive act which would indicate a refusal to return the article, and in Bava Metzia 26b no such act occurred prior to abandonment by the one who lost the object. However, in the ordinary case of withdrawal, the act of withdrawal itself is sufficient to negate the positive command of "you shall give it back to him."

44. There are only two situations where one need not retrieve the lost property of another. The first is where even if it were the finder's property, the finder himself would not retrieve it. For example, if one were an elderly person and the object was of the type that this person would not normally carry in public, one is not under an obligation to treat another's property better than one's own; Shulhan Arukh, Hoshen Mishpat 263:1. Even in that situation, Jewish law encourages one to retrieve the object or pay the person whose object one did not salvage. Shulhan Arukh, Hoshen Mishpat on id. The second case is when one lost an object of one's own, and in the process of search, one finds one's own lost object and the lost object of another, and one cannot take both objects, one may retrieve one's own object first; See Dinnai Mammonut, supra note 3, at 8:3.

45. Pithei Hoshen, supra note 3, at 1:3(n.8); Israel Meir Kagan, Mishnah Berurah 443:12; Elijah of Villna, Biur HaGra Hoshen Mishpat 348:22.

46. Shulhan Arukh, Hoshen Mishpat 259:1; Pithei Hoshen, supra note 3, at 1:5.

47. Pithei Hoshen, supra note 3, at 2:11-14; Childs, supra note 34, at 337 (pp. 452-453).

48. Dinnai Mammonut, supra note 3, at 1:9. One of the most interesting applications of the rules of returning lost property can be found in Joseph Babad, Minhat Hinuch, Commandment 339 who seems to maintain that the rules of returning lost property provide guidance about when one is obligated to save a person's spiritual well being. He maintains that this is an a forcia situation as compared to returning lost property.

49. Bava Meziah 31a.

50. Ibid; Shulhan Arukh, Hoshen Mishpat 267:1. Moses Maimonides, stating the rule allowing return without informing the owner, makes the following comment: "[h]e also has fulfilled the mitzvah;" Mishnah Torah, Theft and Abandonment, 11:16. David Halevy, Turei Zahav (Taz), Shulhan Arukh, Hoshen Mishpat 267:1 argues that Maimonides' choice of language indicates that return without informing the owner, although technically acceptable, is not preferred.

51. Childs, supra note 34, at 333 (page 433).

52. See e.g., Bava Meziah 28a-b; Moses Maimonides, Mishnah Torah, Theft and Abandonment, 13:1-9; Shulhan Arukh, Hoshen Mishpat 267:3 and commentaries; Pithei Hoshen, supra note 3, at 7:5-6.

It seems logical that the precise procedure which one follows to notify members of society that one has found a lost object depends to a great extent on each particular society and its methods of communication. Dinnai Mammonut, supra note 3, at 3:1; Shulhan Arukh, Hoshen Mishpat 267:3 recounts that one announces in the synagogues. See Dinnai Mammonut, supra note 3, at 3:1(n.1) and Pithei Hoshen, supra note 3, at 7:(n.10), for a discussion of what to do in a society where many do not attend synagogue for worship; see also Moshe Schreiber, Responsa Hatam Sofer, Hoshen Mishpat 122 for a discussion of whether it is appropriate to advertize in a newspaper. In a society in which the government has established a working process to return lost objects to their genuine owner, it would appear that it is appropriate to use that process, as that too is a form of announcement. So too, Moses Isserless states (Shulhan Arukh, Hoshen Mishpat 259:7) that Jewish law accepts a secular determination that one must return a lost object to its owner, even if according to Jewish law it would be permissible to keep the object (such as after abandonment). It is unclear, however, if secular law can abrogate the obligation according to Jewish law in a situation where the secular law is more lenient than the Jewish law; Pithei Hoshen, supra note 3, at 2:(53).

53. Shulhan Arukh, Hoshen Mishpat 265:1; and Zalman of Lydia, Shulhan Arukh Harav, Hoshen Mishpat 265:33; Pithei Hoshen, supra note 3, at 8:1-2.

54. Childs, supra note 34, at 333.

55. Finding Lost Goods, 36A Corpus Juris Secundum 7 [Hereinafter Goods, C.J.S.]; Zech v. Accola, 253 Wis. 80, 33 N.W. 2d 232 (Wis. 1948); Manufacturers Safe Deposit Co. v. Cohen, 193 Misc. 900, 85 N.Y.S.2d 650 (N.Y. Sup., 1948) reversed on other grounds, In re Cohen's Estate, 98 N.Y.S.2d 197 (N.Y.A.D. 1950).

56. Laws of New York, supra note 5, at 252

57. Laws of New York, supra note 5, at 252.

58. Laws of New York, supra note 5, at 253 describe in great detail the obligations of the police, which include "the police . . . shall accept and retain custody of the property" and "the police . . . shall give to the person depositing it a receipt" and "if at any time the police have reason to believe that a person has an interest in found property or in a found instrument in their possession and reason to know his whereabouts, they shall give notice of the finding and deposit and the location of the office to which the property or instrument is transmitted to such person."

59. Moses Maiminides, Mishnah Torah Stolen or Abandoned Property 13:10.

60. Ray Brown, Law of Personal Property (3rd. Ed., 1975) at page 24.

61. Some authorities have stated that there is one mechanism to acquire such title. Jacob Lorberbaum, Netivot Hamishpat 256:1 notes that according to Jewish law, property whose ownership cannot be factually determined does not transfer either through an intestacy inheritance or through a will; thus one could claim that after a period of time has elapsed such that the original owner who lost the property is certainly deceased, the possessor at that time would acquire the property; see also Pithei Hoshen, supra note 3, at 7:(n.10) for a similar idea. It is interesting to note that a similar distinction has been advanced by American courts; see Burdick v. Chesebrough, 94 A.D. 532, 88 N.Y.S. 13 (N.Y.A.D. 1904).

62. Shabtai ben Meir HaCohen (Shakh), commenting on Shulhan Arukh, Hoshen Mishpat 222:5, 267:17, 300:10; Jacob Lorberbaum, Netivot Hamishpat 76:5; Moshe Schreiber, Hatam Sofer, Hoshen Mishpat 122. See also the discussion of this topic by Pithei Hoshen, supra note 3, at Laws of Loans 7:(n.32, 36) and Laws of Lost Property, 7:(n.10). See also text accompanying notes 18 to 22.

63. This understanding of the "let the object reside" rule is limited to those situations where the possessor acquired possession properly; all agree that in situations where he did not acquire possession properly, he has no rights to use the object at all, and the object remains unowned.

64. The term "decisors" is the conventional translation used to denote those who decide Jewish law, in Hebrew poskim, literally "those who decide." Moses Feinstein, Iggerot Moshe Hoshen Misphat 2:45(4); Eliezer Waldenburg, Tzitz Eliezer 12:88. This has also been phrased in a slightly different manner. Based on Tosaphot, Bava Kama 66a, some wish to assert that the finder of the item owes an inchoate debt to the original owner, but that the item itself belongs to the finder after abandonment occurs. According to this approach, the finder would "purchase" the item from the original owner, and would be required to pay its value to the original owner should he come forward. See Hayyim Auerbach, Divrai Mishpat 260:1 who discusses this issue; see also comments of Abraham Isaiah Karlitz, Hazon Ish, Bava Kama 18:1 who notes that this approach cannot be harmonized with Jewish law's obligation to pick the lost item up as a bailment for its original owner.

65. This seems to be the opinion of Karo and Isserless, both of whom indicate that this property is held by the court, and not by a person; see Shulhan Arukh, supra note 11, at 300:1 and comments of Isser Zalmal Meltzer, Even HaAzel, Laws of Claims and Claimants, appendix to section 76; Hayyim Halberstam Divrai Hayyim, Claim and Claimants, 21.

66. Goods, C.J.S. supra note 54, at 2.

67. id.

68. Goods, C.J.S. supra note 54, at 3.

69. New York v. Haws, 56 N.Y. 175 (18??); Goods, C.J.S. supra note 54, at 3.

70. Laws of New York, supra note 5, at 257.

71. Essentially the law requires that the police notify people who they reasonably think might own the property and that they notify the public of the loss so that the true finder can reclaim the property. After a period of time which varies depending on the value of the object (less than $100, three months; less than $500, six months; less than $5000, one year; more than $5000, three years) the finder can claim title. Laws of New York, supra note 5, at 252.

72. Bava Meziah 93a; Moses Maimonides, Mishnah Torah, Hiring [of Workers], 1:1-2.

73. Bava Meziah 29a; Cf. Bava Kama 56b.

74. A note on the titles of books in the Jewish legal tradition is needed, if for no other reason than to explain why the single most significant work of Jewish law written in the last 500 years, the Shulhan Arukh, should have a name which translates into English as "The Set Table." Unlike the tradition of most Western law, in which the

titles to scholarly publications reflect the topics of the works, the tradition in Jewish legal literature is that a title rarely names the relevant subject. Instead, the title usually consists either of a pun based on the title of an earlier work on which the current writing comments or of a literary phrase into which the authors' names have been worked (sometimes in reliance on literary license).

A few examples demonstrate each phenomenon. Rabbi Jacob ben Asher's classical treatise on Jewish law was entitled "The Four Pillars" (Arba Turim), because it classified all of Jewish law into one of four areas (see note 1 for more on this). A major commentary on this work that, to a great extent, supersedes the work itself is called "the House of Joseph" (Beit Yosef), since it was written by Rabbi Joseph Karo. Once Karo's commentary (i.e., the house) was completed, one could hardly see "The Four Pillars" it was built on. A reply commentary by Rabbi Joel Sirkes, designed to defend "The Four Pillars" from Karo's criticisms, is called "The New House" (Bayit Hadash). Sirkes proposed his work (i.e., the new house) as a replacement for Karo's prior house. When Rabbi Karo wrote his own treatise on Jewish law, he called it "The Set Table" (Shulhan Arukh) which was based on (i.e., located in) "The House of Joseph." Rabbi Isserles' glosses on "The Set Table"- which were really intended vastly to expand "The Set Table" - are called "The Tablecloth," because no matter how nice the table is, once the tablecloth is on it, one hardly notices the table. Rabbi David Halevi's commentary on the Shulhan Arukh was named the "Golden Pillars" (Turai Zahav) denoting an embellishment on the "legs" of the "Set Table." This type of humorous interaction continues to this day in terms of titles of commentaries on the classical Jewish law work, the Shulhan Arukh.

Additionally, there are book titles that are mixed literary puns, and biblical verses. For example, Rabbi Shabtai ben Meir HaCohen wrote a very sharp critique on the above mentioned Turai Zahav ("Golden Pillars"), which he entitled Nekudat Hakesef, "Spots of Silver," which is a veiled misquote of the verse in Song of Songs 1:11 which states "we will add bands of gold to your spots of silver" (turai zahav al nekudat hakesef, with the word turia "misspelled.") Thus, HaCohen's work is really "The Silver Spots on the Golden Pillars," with the understanding that it is the silver that appears majestic when placed against an all gold background.)

Other works follow the model of incorporating the name of the scholar into the work. For example, the above mentioned Rabbi Shabtai ben Meir HaCohen's commentary on the Shulhan Arukh itself is entitled Seftai Kohen "the words of the Kohen," (a literary embellishment of "Shabtai HaCohen," the author's name). Rabbi Moses Feinstein's collection of responsa are called Iggerot Moshe, "Letters from Moses." To make life even more complex, the rabbinic tradition frequently shorted names into acronyms, making their true origins even more obscure. Thus, the work named Seftai Cohen, is actually referred to in the Jewish law literature by its acronym, Shakh, confusing its origins even further. Indeed, most acronyms begins with the same letter — R — as most authorities were known by their titled name, which began wit the word "rabbi."

Of course, a few leading works of Jewish law are entitled in a manner that informs the reader of their content. Thus, the Fourteenth Century Spanish sage, Nahmanides (Ramban) wrote a work on issues in causation entitled "Indirect Causation in [Jewish] Tort Law" (Dina Degarmei) and the modern Jewish law scholar Eliav Schochatman's classical work on civil procedure in Jewish law is named Seder Hadin ("Arranging the Case,") a modern Hebrew synonym for civil procedure.

75. Moses Maimonides, Mishnah Torah, Theft and Abandonment 13:10; Shulhan Arukh, Hoshen Mishpat 267:16.

76. Shulhan Arukh, Hoshen Mishpat 267:16.

77. Both Joshua Falk-Cohen and Shabtai ben Meir HaCohen label this dispute as a case of legal doubt; see comments their comments on id.

78. For a detailed discussion of how and why Jewish law resolves certain financial disputes in this matter, see Oded Lipa Levfar, Mishpetei ha-Migo (2nd ed., Benei Brak, 1993).

79. Dinnai Mammonut, supra note 3, 4:1.

80. Bava Kama 56b.

81. Obviously the mere fact that the object is in the finder's possession does not constitute involvement in a mitzvah (esek bemitzvah). The bailee must actually be involved in preserving the object. See Tosafot, Bava Kama 56b.

82. Providing charity for a person's daily food needs is mandatory in Jewish law; see Shulhan Arukh, Yoreh Deah 250:1.

83. This distant definition of benefit is not foreign to American law. Frequently, the law defines even a very tangential theoretical benefit as sufficient to be classified as a benefit as a matter of law. See e.g. Donovan v. Bierwirth, 680 F.2d 263 (2nd Cir. 1982) (For the purposes ERISA law, a benefit encompasses even situations where there is no apparent real financial benefit).

84. Goods, C.J.S. supra note 54, at 7(b) (and particularly notes 79,80,80.5).

85. See e.g. Ray Brown, Personal Property, supra note 7, at p.30-31; Goods, C.J.S. supra note 54, at 7(b).

86. The New York State recodification of the law made this issue moot, as the finder does not hold the item at all; that duty now falls on the police. The police may not use the property and have no ownership interest in it although it is unclear what type of bailment (if any) is created; see 24 Op.State Compt. 445, 1968 (a town may not use valuable lost and found property in its recreation program) and Fuentes v. Wendt, 106 Misc. 1030, 436 N.Y.S.2d 801 (1981) (finder of bonds was entitled to award of $75,000, which was value of bonds, and entitled to interest commencing from date police department had improperly refused to deliver bonds to finder.)

87. Tosafot, Bava Meziah 31b; Shulhan Arukh, Hoshen Mishpat 265:1.

88. Rav Brown, Personal Property, supra note 7, at p.31; Goods, C.J.S. supra note 54, at 4; Automobile Ins. Co. v. Kirby, 25 Ala. App. 245, 145 So. 123 (Ala App. 1932). At common law if the owner has offered a reward, the return of the lost property by the finder constitutes the performance of a [unilateral] contract and enables him to recover the amount stipulated. This is accepted as well in Jewish law, although it is perhaps limited only to the area of lost property; Joshua Falk-Cohen, Sefer Meirat Ainayim Shulhan Arukh, Hoshen Mishpat 265:6-7.

89. Moses Maimonides, Mishnah Torah, Theft and Abandonment 12:4; Shulhan Arukh, Hoshen Mishpat 264:3-5; Goods, C.J.S., supra note 54, at 4.

90. Ray Brown, Personal Property, supra note 7, at p.31. The leading case is Reader v. Anderson's 4 Dana (Ky.) 196 (1836) which states: "It seems to us that there is an implied request from the owner to all other persons to endeavor to secure to him lost property which he is anxious to retrieve; and that, therefore there should be an implied undertaking to (at least) indemnify any person, who shall, by the expenditure of time or money contribute to a reclamation of the lost property."

91. Ibid. Of course it would not be reasonable if the loss exceeds the value of the object.

92. As explained above, Jewish law would not require a worker to take such time off; if he did, compensation would be appropriate.

93. Bava Meziah 30b.

94. Ibid. at 31b.

95. Moses Maimonides, Mishnah Torah, Theft and Abandonment 12:4.

96. Shulhan Arukh, Hoshen Mishpat 265:1.

97. Moses Isserless (Rama), Shulhan Arukh, Hoshen Mishpat 264:5.

98. See comments of Jacob ben Asher (Tur), Moses Isserless (Rama), and Shabtai ben Meir (Shakh) all commenting on Shulhan Arukh, Hoshen Mishpat 264:4 and Pithei Hoshen, supra note 3, at 8:(n.10).

99. New York law allows payment of expenses to the state for state incurred expenses. However, unlike either the common law or Jewish law, such expenses were, in effect, paid by the finder since it was the finder in whom title vested. New York law allowed only expense reimbursement, and only of expenses directly relating to the item itself;

see Laws of New York, supra note 5, at 253 ("expenses of taking of custody, transportation, storage and appraisal, any special expense incurred in giving notice, and any other special expense attributable to administration of this article with respect to the particular property"). However, the finder was entitled to no expense reimbursement should the true owner come forward.

100. See supra, sections IV-V.

101. See material discussed infra in text accompanying notes 101 to 111.

102. As explained, infra text accompanying note 103, this second category is called simanim in Hebrew, and it literally means signals or marks.

103. Ibid., and Bava Meziah 27b. According to those authorities who rule simanim (marks or symbols) to be a biblically sufficient form of identification, this requirement is traced to the words "and so shalt thou do with his garment;" just as the garment is unique in that it contains marks or symbols, so too any lost object which may be identified through marks or symbols must be returned. If symbols without eyewitness correlation is merely rabbinic, the biblical specification of "garment" has reference to claimants who may claim the article not by virtue of identification furnished by symbols or marks but through the testimony of witnesses, which certainly suffices.

104. Furthermore, as explained in text accompanying notes 109, Jewish law provided other means of isolating the potential thief. Practically, it is of no consequence in the ordinary law of lost property why one conclude the symbols or marks are efficacious. In either event, one claiming to be the rightful owner can recover from the finder by furnishing adequate such symbols or marks. The significance of this discussion is of practical relevance in connection with other areas of Jewish law — for example, the court's decision allowing a woman whose husband has disappeared the right to remarry on the ground that a dead body has been identified as that of her husband.

105. Rabbi Solomon ben Meir (Rashba) and Rabbenu Nissim (Ran) on Bava Meziah 27b; Vidal of Tolosa, Maggid Mishnah, Theft and Abandonment 13:3; Shabtia ben Meir (Shakh) commenting on Shulhan Arukh, Hoshen Mishpat 267:2.

106. The different categories of marks or symbols is fully explained in Dinnai Mammonut, supra note 3, at 3:2.

107. Such symbols will definitely suffice to recover lost property and therefore preclude any presumption of abandonment.

108. For a listing of various types of marks, see Pithei Hoshen, supra note 3, at 5:1-15. It is clear however, that a collection of insignificant symbols, can, in composite, become significant. Thus, one may not return a lost red shirt to a person who states that he too lost a red shirt, since there are many red shirts in the world; so too, one cannot return a lost shirt which is size 15 to a person who states he lost a size 15 shirt. The same is true about sleeve size. One could however return a shirt to a person who identified that he lost a size 15 red shirt with 28 inch sleeve if such garments are uncommon. Many of these determinations are contextual, see e.g. Pithei Hoshen, supra note 3, at 5:1 ("any item which has a mark that makes the item different from other similar items such that the loser of the item can recognize that it is his ...").

Jewish law also recognized that — at least in theory — even an item without a clear mark can be returned to an owner who claims them if he says that he clearly recognizes the item as his, if the person is a recognized Torah scholar known not to speak in haste. Shulhan Arukh, Hoshen Mishpat supra note 11, at 262:21. There is a dispute between David Halevy (Taz) and Joshua Falk-Cohen (Sema) about whether any post-talmudic Torah scholars fall within this classification; compare their comments on id.

109. Shulhan Arukh, Hoshen Mishpat supra note 11, at 267:4.

110. Shulhan Arukh, Hoshen Mishpat 267:6 and comments of Joshua Falk-Cohen (Sema) on id. Those authorities who rule that symbols and signs work on a biblical level, rule that one returns lost items even to a thief when he provides true symbols. Others rule that a thief needs to present witnesses to get back his own lost property; see Pithei Hoshen, supra note 3, at 7:10.

111. Dougherty v. Norlin 147 Kan. 565, 78 P.2d 65, 66 (Kan. 1938); Wood v. Pierson, 45 Mich. 313, 7 N.W. 888 (Mich. 1881); Goods, C.J.S. supra note 54, at 8a.

112. Fisher v. Klingenberger, 576 N.Y.S.2d 476, 478 (N.Y. Civ. Ct., 1991). Defendant in this case returned the object to a

person who provided clear symbols (according to Jewish Law) but yet was actually a thief aware of the find. The court recounted:

[A]n unidentified man had approached him in the parking lot next to the F.B.O. building. The man stated he was the owner of lost airplane tools, and he then satisfactorily described to [defendant] the contents of the toolbag. Whereupon, [defendant] accepted the unidentified man's claim of title and surrendered the tools to him then and there. The transcript of [defendant's] testimony on this point is:

Q. (You gave up the tools) without asking for identification, or for his name?

A. There was no need to do that. He knew what I had. I believed they were his. I would not have known him anyway. I was glad to get rid of them. I just wanted to get rid of them.

These facts explain the Sages requirement that the person identify himself as an honorable person before claiming lost goods as his own, even if a symbol is provided.

113. Literally, avudah mikkol adam, "lost to the whole world". Bava Meziah 22b. See Rabbi Solomon Yitzhaki (Rashi), Bava Kama 66a, who asserts that this case, a Tannaitic interpretation of Deuteronomy 22:13 is the Biblical source for the principle of abandonment in lost property. For a longer discussion of this issue, see J. David Bleich, The Controversy Concerning the Sotheby Sale, Cardozo Law Review 8:91 (1986).

114. Shulhan Arukh, Hoshen Mishpat supra note 11, at 259:7; Joshua Falk-Cohen (Sema) commenting on id.

115. Moses Maimonides, Mishnah Torah Theft and Abandonment 11:10.

116. Shulhan Arukh, Hoshen Mishpat 259:7.

117. Bava Meziah 24b; Shulhan Arukh, Hoshen Mishpat 259:7.

118. Commentary of Asher ben Yeheil on Bava Meziah 24b.

119. Joshua Falk Cohen (Sema), Shulhan Arukh, Hoshen Mishpat 259:7.

120. Literally "zuto shel yam," the classic talmudic case of destruction.

121. Childs, supra note 34, at 335 (p449).

122. Personal Property, supra note 7, at p.31.

123. Laws of New York, supra note 5, at 251 ("The term "property" as used in this article means money, instruments payable, drawn or issued to bearer or to cash, goods, chattels and tangible personal property other than . . . wrecks governed by the provisions of the navigation law . . .").

124. Davidson v. State, 514 N.Y.S.2d 615, 1987 A.M.C. 2483 (Ct. Cl., 1987) (State brought action to determine ownership of two 1,000-pound bronze cannon cast in 1748. The cannon were discovered by skin divers in a lake. Court awarded skin divers $34,000 for salvage of cannon).

125. Bava Meziah 24b; Moses Maimonides, Mishnah Torah, Theft and Abandonment 11:7.

126. In Hebrew, lifnim me-shurat hadin.

127. Mordecai ben Hillel on Bava Meziah 257; Meir HaCohen of Rothenberg, Hagaot Mamaniot on Maimonides, supra note 124,; Shabtai ben Meir (Shakh), commenting on Shulhan Arukh, Hoshen Mishpat 259:3.

128. Bava Meziah 30b.

129. All three legal system provide very similar or identical answers to each other in two of the thirteen questions posed, for an overlap of 16%.

Courtesy of Jlaw.com

Finders Keepers? First Impressions and Ancient Wisdom

By Harris Ominsky

Harris Ominsky is a partner in the law firm of Blank Rome Comisky & McCauley LLP, which has offices in Pennsylvania, New York, New Jersey, Delaware, District of Columbia, Maryland, Florida and Ohio. He participates every Saturday morning in a Torah discussion group at Beth David Synagogue in Gladwyne, Pennsylvania.

Finders Keepers
Losers Weepers
—Children's Rhyme

When a construction contractor finds a hidden box of cash and other valuables while working on a farm or in a motel—who owns it? This is one of those ancient property questions discussed in Talmudic and law school classes. Appellate courts have answered that question the same way in two recent cases. Terry v. Lock Hospitality, Inc., 343 Ark. 452 (2001); and Corliss v. Wenner, 2001 WL 1007928 (Idaho App.)

The simplistic answer is that the property belongs to the original owner who hid it there. But if that owner cannot be found, does it belong to the contractor or the real estate owner?

The Motel Ceiling

In Terry v. Lock Hospitality, the contractors were renovating a Best Western Hotel in Conway, Arkansas, when they found a dusty box behind ceiling tiles that contained over $38,000 in old currency. At the time of discovery the owner was in the room and the contractor gave him the box. When the contractor sued to resolve ownership rights, the Arkansas Supreme Court held that the money belongs to the owner of the motel because the circumstances showed that it was property that had been intentionally hidden in the ceiling and apparently forgotten. The Court commented that the issue was one "of first impression" in Arkansas, and relied heavily on an Iowa Supreme Court case that set up four categories for found property:

Abandoned Property: Property discarded with the intention of terminating ownership.

Lost Property: Property unintentionally left because of carelessness or inadvertence.

Mislaid Property: Property intentionally left in a place where the owner can find it and the place is later forgotten.

Treasure Trove: Gold, silver or paper money concealed in the earth or a private place under circumstances indicating that the treasure has been concealed for so long that the owner is likely dead or unknown.

Under these doctrines, the finder of lost or abandoned property and treasure trove has a right of possession against everyone except the rightful owner. However, a finder of mislaid property must turn it over to the landowner, who in turn must safeguard it for the true owner.

The Ranch Driveway

The Idaho Court of Appeals also favored the landowner in the case of Corliss v. Wenner, which was decided on September 5, 2001. It involved a suit by an asphalt-paving contractor who was installing a driveway on a ranch when he unearthed a glass jar containing paper-wrapped rolls of gold coins with a contested value ranging between $30,000-$1,000,000. The coins dated from 1857 to 1914, and the glass jar was estimated to be about 70 years old. As in Arkansas, this was also viewed as a case "of first impression" for Idaho.

After applying an analysis similar to that of the Arkansas court, the Idaho court awarded the coins to the ranch owner, who, theoretically, must hold them for the true owner. The Court noted that only lost or abandoned property should go to the finder because those circumstances involve an element of involuntariness, in contrast with the other categories which involve intentional acts by the true owner in placing the property where it was found.

Modern Trend

The Court held that the "modern trend" favored characterizing the find as mislaid property, under which the right-of-possession goes to the landowner. The coins in this case were not abandoned because the condition in which they were found evidenced an intent to keep them safe. They were not lost since they were secreted with care in a specific place to protect them from the elements and from other people.

The decision analyzed and rejected the ancient rule of treasurer trove which supported the "finders-keepers" rule. This rule was followed by a number of states before 1950; however, the Court cited more current cases throughout the United States that awarded found treasure and coins to the landowner. It concluded that the finders-keepers rule for treasure trove was not even a part of the common law of England as defined by the Idaho Code, Section 73-116, and therefore, that Code did not require that it be adopted under Idaho's law. In a footnote, it quoted one wry commentator on this issue, "The old rule of treasure trove may make good theatre, but it's poor law and its death can come none too soon."

The modern rules are best, but not always easy to apply. The easier rule would be "finders keepers," which would have awarded the found property to the contractors.

Rationale

Some commentators have rationalized the rule of leaving the property with the landowner because that person is more likely to eventually find the original owner. They reason that that owner may someday come back for the property and claim it from the landowner. On the other hand, if the contractor takes it with him, the rightful owner may never locate that property again—or the contractor.

This rationale is somewhat questionable because it is not clear that the landowner has any more of an incentive to try to locate the original owner than the contractor—or to admit that he has the property, if and when the original owner ever shows up.

For that matter, from a philosophical perspective why is a motel owner any more entitled to found property than, say, a former owner of the motel? Suppose the current owner had recently bought a motel from someone that had owned it for many years. Suppose the found property was worth more than the motel itself. Should it be said that the new owner of the motel has any more right to it than the old owner—or the one who owned the motel when the box was left there? Certainly, the parties never intended to transfer the lost property, and any implied intent would have to favor the conclusion that the seller never intended to include it in the sale.

What about lenders? Suppose the motel were encumbered with a mortgage and all of its fixtures, equipment and other property were included in the security agreement and filed financing statements under the Uniform Commercial Code. Would the lender have a claim that any discovered property covered by the UCC should be treated as part of its collateral?

Ancient Wisdom

Ancients struggled with the law of lost property long before the UCC. Rules of return were set up in Deuteronomy:

1) If you see your fellow's ox or sheep gone astray, do not ignore it, you must take it back to your fellow; 2) If your fellow does not live near you or you do not know who he is, you shall bring it home and it shall remain with you until your fellow claims it; then you shall give it back to him; 3) You shall do the same thing with his ass; you shall do the same with his garment; and so too shall you do with anything that your fellow loses and you find: you must not remain indifferent. (Deuteronomy 22.)

The Hebrew Talmud, which includes the Mishnah and the Gemara, was written by scholars and elaborates on the Deuteronomy passage. The Mishnah is a collection of interpretations of biblical passages and laws that were eventually edited in the second century of the Christian Era. The Gemara consists of commentaries on the Mishnah which were edited around the year 380 C.E. in Tiberius and supplemented, around 500, in Babylonia.

The Baba Mezia is the treatise of Talmudic law which includes the law of lost property. The quotes and the references to the Baba Mezia in the following passages are taken from an English translation of the Babylonian Talmud by Rabbi Dr. I. Epstein, Vol. II (London, The Soncino Press 1935).

Much of the Talmudic discourse on ownership of lost property dealt with the ability to identify the original owner and the circumstances under which the property was found. The established rules were similar to those applied in the motel and ranch cases discussed earlier.

The Talmudic law distinguished between those finds that belonged to the finder and other finds that must be "announced" or "proclaimed" so that the original owner may claim them. For example, "scattered money" belonged to the finder because the rabbis thought that money like that could not be identified by the loser and was therefore given up by him as beyond recovery.

Mishnah

On the other hand, the rabbis required the finder to attempt to return those objects that the loser could identify. The Mishnah provides:

The following objects have to be proclaimed: If one finds fruit in a vessel, or a vessel by itself, money in a purse, or a purse by itself; heaps of fruit, heaps of coins, three coins on top of each other, bundles of sheaves in private premises, home-made loaves, fleeces of wool from the craftsman's workshop, jars of wine or jars of oil, they have to be proclaimed. (B.M. 24b-25a).

In that section the rabbis then debated how to handle found coins. Scattered coins belonged to the finder because they could not easily be identified. On the other hand, "heaps of coins" might be identified. For example, Rabbi Isaac maintained that if coins were found arranged in a pyramid fashion, with a large coin at the bottom, a smaller one above it, etc., they must have been placed that way by the owner; and, therefore, the finder must proclaim.

The rabbis then discussed why a single coin which was found would not have to be returned to a claimant. They used the example of a found "Nero coin" or a coin of "such-and-such emperor," and made a fine distinction worthy of the most sophisticated modern legal minds:

Moreover, even if his name is written upon it, his claim is still rejected, because an identification mark is of no avail in respect to a coin, for one can say, he may have expended it and someone else lost it. (B.M. 25a-25b)

The comment also dealt with articles that were found inside of a wall. The Mishnah says:

If he finds [an article] amidst debris or in an old wall, they belong to him. If he finds aught in a new wall: if in the outer half [thereof], it is his; in the inner half, it belongs to the owner of the house. But if it [the house] used to be rented to others, even if he finds [articles] in the house itself, they belong to him. (B.M.25b-26a).

Gemara

On the face of it, the distinctions made in this passage seem rather arbitrary. However, the Gemara sheds some light on the ancient reasoning. The reference to the "outer half" of the wall describes a wall that fronted a public thoroughfare, and the rabbis assumed that the found article must have been placed in the part facing the street by a passer-by who would not return. Therefore, it belonged to the finder. They also assumed the "inner half," which was the part facing the house it enclosed, was a likely hiding place for the owner of the house. Therefore, the owner of the house should have the right to a find in that half.

The other distinction is between an "old wall" and a "new wall." One of the commentators said that the article found in the old wall belongs to the finder because that rule applies only if the find is "exceedingly rusty." The finder can then argue to the owner of the house that the "find belonged to Amorites," who were one of the races that formerly inhabited Palestine and who were no longer there.

The Gemara also explains the rule that favors the finder if the house "used to be rented to others." In this conclusion the rabbis assumed that the finder was the present tenant and they reasoned that before a tenant had left the house, he would have made a thorough search to see that he left nothing behind. One of the sages, Rabbi Shemaiah b. Zé ira, supported his conclusion with a creative and graphic analogy:

What is the reason? Because the streets of Jerusalem were swept daily. This proves that we assume: the earlier [losses] have gone, and these [coins] are different ones. So here too, the earlier [deposits] have gone, and these belong to the last [tenant]. (B.M. 26a-26b)

The Mishnah also emphasizes the importance of identification when determining that a finder must not keep a lost garment, as mentioned in the Deuteronomy passage. The Mishnah states:

The garment too was included in all of these: Why then was it singled out? That an analogy might be drawn therewith, teaching: just as a garment is distinguished in that it bears identification marks and is claimed, so must everything be announced, if it bears identification marks and is claimed. (B.M. 27a)

Returning Property

The Encyclopedia Judaica, Vol. 11, pages 504-506 (Keter Publishing House, Jerusalem Ltd.), summarizes that lost property, called avedah, is property that has passed out of its owner's possession and its whereabouts are unknown to him. Generally, that property must be returned to its rightful owner, but when that owner has clearly abandoned any search for it, his ownership in it ceases and the finder may retain it for himself (B.M. 21b). The finder who improperly appropriates an avedah for himself was considered a thief (B.M. 26b). Some scholars were of the opinion that the finder's degree of responsibility for an avedah, as long as it was in his care, was the same as that of an unpaid bailee, while others equated the standard of care required to that of a paid bailee (B.M. 29a).

Detailed rules were even established about what the finder must do to facilitate returning the found property to the original owner. When the owner's identity was unknown, he must bring the avedah to public notice, i.e., by announcing it. If the claimant-owner offers notable identification marks, the property must be returned to him, but if he is suspected of being an imposter he must produce other evidence of his ownership (B.M. 28b).

Before the destruction of the Temple, the announcement was made from a stone platform in Jerusalem, during the three festivals when the people were gathered there. In later times the announcement was made in synagogues, and it was also decreed that in places where the secular authorities expropriated all lost property, a finder only had to tell his neighbors and acquaintances (B.M. 28(b)). If no claimant responded to the announcement, the finder was required to retain the avedah in trust for the owner, indefinitely.

Other issues sometimes entered into the Talmudic deliberations. The story is told about a respected Rabbi who asked his students: "If a non-Jew sells a camel to a Jew and the buyer finds a valuable jewel hidden in the collar of the camel, who owns the jewel?" The student answered that under Talmudic law the jewel belongs to the finder because neither party knew that it was there, and the owner of the jewel could not be identified. When the Rabbi responded that it belonged to the seller, the student protested, "But you have taught us that under these circumstances the found property belongs to the buyer." "Yes, but in this case," said the Rabbi, "think about what the seller will say about our G-d."

Unstated Premise

When modern courts reach the conclusion that a contractor should not walk away with a valuable find, an implicit assumption may be operating which is not related to whose god will be honored. When you invite a contractor or other business visitor into your building, you would never expect that person to leave with valuable property any more than the ceiling tiles—unless there were some kind of advance arrangement about this. The unstated business premise is that the invitee comes there for a specific purpose, and no other one. A contractor contracts to perform designated work for a specific amount of money. It would seem to be a major distortion of that understanding for the contractor to be able to receive a windfall, which could be worth many times more than the contract price.

Think of it this way. If the law were otherwise, owners should use a standard form AIA construction contract spelling out that if the contractor should discover anything on the property, it belongs to the landowner. You will not see that provision in many construction contracts, and it should not be needed. Under the circumstances in the cited cases, why should the ownership of found property be determined by whether or not we find such language in a contract?

Unsolved Mystery

The big mystery in these types of cases is about the characters who left the valuables originally. Were they hiding ill-gotten gains? Are they still planning to rent the motel room at some time in the future and come back to collect their box? Do they intend to sneak onto the ranch to dig up their jar on some dark night? Are they in jail? Have they been killed? Have they developed Alzheimer's?

In any event, somebody may be out there somewhere who is entitled to large sums of money that are being held by the owners of the properties where they were left. If you are that somebody and happen to read this article, get back as soon as you can to the Wenner Ranch. Or the Conway Best Western Motel. And when you recover your money, don't forget me.

Courtesy of Jlaw.com

Theft of Art During World War II: Its Legal and Ethical Consequences The Jewish Perspective

By Steven H. Resnicoff, Professor, DePaul University College of Law[1]

I. Preliminary Observations

We have already heard about how secular law approaches contests over stolen art. Jewish law—which is a coherent legal system, with axioms, principles, precedents and values—takes a different approach, and this is what I will focus upon.2 Perhaps secular law can profit from Jewish law's insights.

Before launching into this subject, though, I want to make a few comments about what has already been said—or, more poignantly—what has not been said. The preceding articles have focused primarily on disputes between the original owners of stolen art and those who are now in possession. Tragically, however, there is much stolen art for which there may not be any legal claimants. Entire families—indeed, entire towns, villages and cities—were cruelly liquidated. Distant relatives, if any survived, may be totally unaware of what specific pieces of art were owned by those who died. Even where original owners survived, they may simply lack the requisite proof to establish their prior ownership of the art.

In many of these cases, however, it may be possible to prove that the art came from some Jewish source—whether from an individual or from a communal organization, such as a looted synagogue. As an ethical matter, what should happen to this art? Should the party in possession (whether a museum or private collector) be entitled to keep it? Or, instead, should this art be used to benefit Jews—either Jewish Holocaust survivors, Holocaust organizations (such as Yad VaShem) or particularized Jewish communities? The Einsatzstab Reichsleiter Rosenberg (the "ERR") had a specific policy of confiscating the art collections of Jews. If the property was stolen because it was owned by Jews qua Jews and the property cannot be returned to its owners (because they perished), perhaps it or its value should be used for Jews. Or perhaps even the answer to this question should depend on whether the current possessor of the property sincerely investigated its provenance before investing in it. After all, this is also part of the totality of any equitable calculus.

Under the law in many lands, where there is no heir, a decedent's property escheats to the state. Should this be the rule regarding Holocaust art? In the case of the Holocaust, a number of countries—and considerable segments of their citizenries—were culpably involved—directly or indirectly—in the murderous elimination of such heirs. Should these countries and citizenries profit from their war crimes?3

Interestingly, immediately after World War II, a significant amount of unclaimed cultural items under American control was distributed to Jewish communities throughout the world by an entity essentially organized for this purpose, the Jewish Restitution Commission, with the approval of the Office of Military Government, U.S. Zone.4 Similarly, in 1996, the Austrian government auctioned off unclaimed World War II art in its possession and used the proceeds for the benefit of Holocaust victims.5 Such procedures obvious raise difficult questions as to precisely which Jewish interests should benefit. Nevertheless, it seems at least intuitively clear that this art be used to promote Jewish interests rather than non-Jewish interests—especially as to art that has Jewish cultural significance, such as religious manuscripts or ritual objects or ornaments.6

II: Jewish Law and the Recovery of Stolen Property

Initially, I should stress that there is an internal Jewish law doctrine known as dina demalkhuta dina (literally, "the law of the kingdom is the law"). This doctrine provides that, under certain circumstances, Jewish law accepts particular secular laws as religiously binding. The precise parameters of this doctrine are subject to considerable debate.7 In any event, for our comparative law purposes, it is more interesting to examine Jewish law's internal rules. Perhaps they can inform the debate as to what secular law should be.8

There are at least three fundamental differences between the principal secular law approaches and Jewish law. First, litigation in common law jurisdictions, such as the United States, usually centers on statute of limitations issues.9 If there is no statute of limitations problem, the original owner wins and the party in possession loses. Under Jewish law no statute of limitations applies to the recovery of stolen property.10

Second, litigation in non-common law jurisdictions, including most European countries, typically revolves around whether the party in possession obtained the property in good faith, without knowing or having reason to know that the property had been stolen.11 If it did, the party in possession wins, and the original owner loses. Under Jewish law, whether a person acquiring stolen property knows it was stolen is also important, but, as we shall soon see, its importance is limited.

Third, aside from these doctrinal differences between the Jewish and secular legal approaches, there is a basic difference as to result. The secular result—at least as between the party in possession and the original owner—is "all or nothing." The common law jurisdictions award "all" to the original owner, while the non-common law jurisdictions award "all" to the good faith purchaser. In sharp contrast, Jewish law provides for a "compromise."

To explain the Jewish law position, it is necessary to introduce a new concept, known as ye'ush (despair). Although this concept is ignored by secular law, it is critical to Jewish law. Ye'ush occurs if and when the original owner of a piece of property despairs of the possibility that he or his heirs will ever recover it.12 Whether ye'ush has occurred in a particular case can be determined either by evidence of the owner's express statements or by operation of law.13 Someone who has possession of stolen goods can only convey title to a good faith transferee if there is ye'ush.14 Consequently, if someone buys stolen goods from a thief and there is no ye'ush, the buyer does not acquire title even if he made the purchase in good faith. As a result, the buyer must surrender the object to its owner.15 In this way, Jewish law differs from the secular law of non-common law countries.

To prevent this rule from obstructing commerce by frightening potential purchasers, ancient Jewish sages decreed that the owner must pay the buyer the amount the buyer paid for the property.16 In the context of stolen art, where market prices may have risen sharply, this would admittedly impose some burden on the buyer, but only as to the loss of possible profit on the purchase of the stolen property. Moreover, the buyer has in the meantime enjoyed possession of the art for free.17

Thus, in a case without ye'ush (i.e., where the original owner has not despaired of recovering his property), common law jurisdictions would rule that the original owner gets the property back and the good faith purchaser gets nothing so long as there is no statute of limitations problem. By contrast, non-common law jurisdictions would say that the good faith purchaser keeps the property and the original owner receives nothing. By contrast, Jewish law provides some relief for the owner and for the good faith purchaser. The original owner recovers his property, and the good faith purchaser, who has enjoyed the property in the meantime, recovers his purchase price.

What about a bad faith purchaser? Under Jewish law, where there has been no ye'ush, a bad faith buyer has the same duty as a good faith buyer to return the property to its original owner. If the buyer purchased the property knowing that it was stolen, the original owner is not obligated to compensate the buyer at all.18 In fact, some Jewish law authorities say this is the case even if the buyer did not know that the property was stolen so long as the seller was a known thief.19 Consequently, as to bad faith buyers before ye'ush, the Jewish law result approximates that of common law and non-common law states.

On the other hand, suppose someone in good faith buys stolen property and there is ye'ush, i.e., the original owner has despaired of ever regaining the property. In such a case, the buyer obtains title to the property.20 Just as in a non-common law jurisdiction, such a buyer would be entitled to keep the property. Nevertheless, even in this scenario, some Jewish law authorities would require the good faith buyer to pay the original owner the difference between the value of the object and the amount that the buyer paid for it.21 In light of possible appreciation in the value of art—as well as the possibly depressed price paid by the buyer22—such a rule could provide the original owner considerable compensation. Thus, at least according to these authorities, Jewish law again mandates a compromise, while the secular systems provide for "all or nothing" results.

Interestingly, however, application of these Jewish law basic rules would provide that if there was ye'ush, a buyer acquires title even if he purchased the property knowing that it was stolen, and he would not technically be obligated to return the property.23 Such a buyer, however. would be required to pay the full the original owner the full market value of the property.24

Up to now, we have surveyed the basic Jewish law rules. There is, however, an overarching principle that urges Jews to do more than the minimum required. While the corresponding secular expression might be to go "beyond the letter of the law," the Jewish expression is to go "within the scope of the law" (lifnim mi-shurat ha-din). This phraseology is said to reflect the notion that the real self is one of kindness. The law defines the maximum distance a person is permitted to stray from his core values. By doing more kindness than is technically required, a person draws closer to his essential self. Under Jewish law, a firmly established custom has the effect of law. According to a number of authorities, a custom developed among Jews—arguably based on the lifnim mi-shurat ha-din principle25—that, even in cases in which there was ye'ush, one who buys stolen property must return it to the original owner if the owner reimburses him for the amount the buyer paid for it.26 Although the buyers in such instances technically obtained title to the stolen goods and were not strictly required to return them, Jews accepted upon themselves the duty to restore the property to those from whom it was stolen.

Notwithstanding this custom, there are various reasons why, under Jewish law, it remains important to determine whether the original owner experienced ye'ush (i.e., whether he despaired of ever regaining possession of his property). For example, it is unclear whether Jewish law would require non-Jews to comply with this custom. Jewish law might not compel non-Jews to do more than the legal minimum. Indeed, even if there existed a validly constituted rabbinic governing authority, it is uncertain whether it would specifically enforce the custom, or whether compliance would depend on the individual's voluntary commitment to conduct himself in accordance with Jewish law.

III. Special Factors Affecting an Analysis of Holocaust Issues

The organized theft of art by Nazis during World War II differed qualitatively from simple theft. From a comparative law perspective, it is noteworthy that, while secular legal discussions do not always account for these differences doctrinally, Jewish law does. For example,27 Jewish law recognizes that, under certain circumstances and to a certain extent, ownership rights may be acquired by the "right of conquest" (kibush milhamah). Although this doctrine appears irrelevant to some cases of stolen art, such as when Jews were betrayed by private Gentile collectors to whom they entrusted their holdings, it seems at least arguably relevant to some of the organized Nazi confiscations. A number of subsidiary issues then arises, for instance, as to whether kibush milhamah operates even if there is no ye'ush, whether kibush milhamah applies to actions taken by a government against its own nationals, and whether an equitable obligation exists to return property which came into one's hands after kibush milhamah.28

On a more elementary level, the plight of Jewish refugees is relevant when evaluating whether the original owners of the stolen art experienced ye'ush. Although in Talmudic times there were various general principles as to when ye'ush might be implied by law, modern commentators suggest that, because of changed circumstances, those principles are no longer valid, and that ye'ush occurred in a particular case would require a highly fact-sensitive inquiry.29

J. David Bleich is a law professor and a contemporary halakhic authority. Rabbi Bleich disagrees with Rabbi Isaac Liebes, another contemporary authority, regarding whether, as a matter of Jewish law, one should generally conclude that Jews caught up in the Holocaust experienced ye'ush as to Hebrew manuscripts that were stolen from them. The following words of Rabbi Bleich serve as apt testimony to the courage and faith of many of the members of the Holocaust generation, whose lives—as well as whose art—were so ruthlessly despoiled:

Rabbi [Isaac] Liebes [author of Teshuvot Bet Avi states]: "In such a state, if they already despaired of their lives, did they not most certainly [despair] of their property? To whom would it occur to think thoughts of his house or fortune while under the nails of the angel of death, the impure foul oppressor, in the death camps and in the ghettos?" Despite its ringing eloquence, this argument is less than compelling. The diabolical designs of the Nazis are now a matter of historical record. But whether or not they were recognized at the time by the intended victims is an entirely different matter. The historical record indicates that the Germans did everything possible to conceal their malevolent intentions from both the victims and the world at large. Moreover, there is certainly every reason to assume that, even in the darkest hours of the Holocaust, the oppressed victims hoped and prayed for the defeat of the Germans at the hands of the Allies, and hence had reason to anticipate that their property would eventually be reclaimed by them or their heirs. Furthermore, even had the nefarious "final solution" been announced to the intended victims, ye'ush would not have ensued. Ye'ush is a psychological phenomenon and it is unthinkable that Jews of the Holocaust generation would have been so lacking in faith as to believe that, in violation of His covenant with Israel, G-d would permit the annihilation of the entire Jewish community. Hence, the unfortunate victims would certainly have clung to the belief that the plundered books would ultimately find their way into Jewish hands. Indeed, that belief has been confirmed by history.30

As time progresses, the generation of corrupt dealers and collectors who collaborated with the Nazis will eventually die out and their holdings, through auctions and the like, will increasingly pass into the public eye. As information, especially from former Soviet bloc countries becomes more accessible, and as Jewish and non-Jewish organizations utilize technologically advanced methods of searching and sharing information, one can hope—and pray—that history confirms such faith.

Notes

1. B.A., Princeton University, 1974; J.D., Yale Law School, 1978; Rabbinic Degree, Beth Medrash Govoha, 1983; Chair (1998-99), Section on Jewish Law, Association of American Law Schools. © 2001, All rights reserved, Steven H. Resnicoff. A version of this article was previously published in Volume X (Fall 1999) of the DePaul University College of Law Journal of Art and Entertainment Law. This article is based on a presentation made at a Symposium entitled, "Theft of Art During World War II: Its Legal and Ethical Consequences," that was sponsored by that journal.

2. Of course, a more comprehensive treatment of the Jewish perspective would require consideration of various additional questions. For example, is it likely, on balance, to be either beneficial or harmful to the Jewish community as a whole (whether in the short-run or in the long-run) for Jewish individuals or organizations to pursue recovery of stolen art, reparations for unpaid wages and similar claims? Does the answer to this question depend on the particular nature of the claims asserted (stolen art versus unpaid wages), the manner in which the claims are asserted (politically versus legally), or the persons or entities against whom the claims are asserted? Second, assuming there were a clear answer to the first question, to what extent should that answer influence an individual Jew or Jewish organization in deciding whether to pursue such a recovery? Admittedly, these are meaningful questions. Alas, the answer to the first (as to the likelihood of communal benefit of harm) is impossible to divine, leaving a discussion of the second a bit overly theoretical.

3. See Michael J. Kurtz, Inheritance of Jewish Property, 20 Cardozo L. Rev. 625 (1998) (mentioning that this argument was raised by Jewish leaders near the end of World War II).

4. Id.

5. See Robert Schwartz, The Limits of the Law: A Call for A New Attitude Toward Artwork Stolen During World War II, 32 Colum. J.L. & Soc. Probs. 1, 25-26 (1998).

6. It is also important to note that while this symposium focuses on stolen art, other types of property were stolen as well. Granted, the problems of proof may be more difficult regarding such other property, and the possibility of feasible solutions may be far more complex. Nevertheless, the loss of all types of property—and

their possible ultimate recovery—remain important from any "Jewish" perspective. Indeed, while lost art may be directly relevant to Jewish families which were once affluent, the loss of other properties—from homes to Shabbos candle-holders—was experienced by virtually all European Jewry.

7. See generally, Michael J. Broyde and Steven H. Resnicoff, Jewish Law and Modern Business Structures: The Corporate Paradigm, 43 Wayne L.Rev. 1685, 1765-1773 (1997); Steven H. Resnicoff, Bankruptcy-A Viable Halachic Option?, Journal of Halacha & Contemporary Society XXIV:5 (Fall 1992). Dina demalkhuta dina would not, for instance, legitimize the discriminatory edicts issued by the Third Reich. For a reference-although an arguably ambiguous reference-to the application of Dina demalkhuta dina to the context of returning stolen property, see Shulhan Arukh, Hoshen Mishpat 353:3. The Shulhan Arukh was authored in the sixteenth century by R. Yosef Caro. Throughout the years, the views of scores of outstanding commentaries have been annotated to the Shulhan Arukh which has contributed to its status as the most central code of Jewish law.

8. For purposes of brevity and clarity my comments about Jewish law's internal rules may include some over-simplification.

9. See, e.g., Robert Schwartz, The Limits of the Law: A Call for a new Attitude Toward Artwork Stolen during World War II, 32 Colum. J.L. & Soc. Probs. 1, 4-5 (1998); Laura McFarland-Taylor, Tracking Stolen Artworks on the Internet: A New Standard for Due Diligence, 16 J. Marshall J. Computer & Info. L. 937, 946-951 (1998); Alexandre A. Montagu, Recent Cases on the Recovery of Stolen Art - The Tug of War Between Owners and Good Faith Purchasers Continues, 18 Colum.-VLA J.L. & Arts 75 (1993). See also Lawrence M. Kaye, Looted Art: What Can and Should Be Done, 20 Cardozo L. Rev. 657, 668 (1998) (arguing that Article I of the 1968 Convention on the Non-Applicability of Statutory Limitations to War Crimes and Crimes Against Humanity, ratified by Russia and a number of Eastern European countries - but not by the United States or other major Western countries - would prevent the assertion of statutes of limitations against civil cases to recover plundered art).

10. Various Jewish law sources, old and new, assert that the mere passage of time does not generally prevent a claimant from successfully asserting his claim. See, e.g., Shulhan Arukh, Hoshen Mishpat 98:1; R. Yehiel Michel Epstein (19th-20th centuries), Arukh ha-Shulhan, Hoshen Mishpat 98:1; R. Ezra Basri (contemporary), Dinei Mamanot I, at 65-66; R.Yaakov Reicher (1670-1733), Shevut Yaakov III:182; R. Yitzhak b. Sheshes (1326-1407), Shut 404. But see Menachem Elon (contemporary), Jewish Law: History, Sources, Principles IV, at 1724-1726 (contending that statutes of limitations have more generally become part of Jewish law).

11. See, generally, the sources cited in note 9, supra.

12. J. David Bleich, Contemporary Halakhic Problems III, at 352.

13. With respect to some types of property, such as Jewish books or manuscripts, there may be legal presumptions against a finding of ye'ush. The applicability of such a presumption in the context of the Holocaust is subject to a spirited debate. See, generally, J. David Bleich, Contemporary Halakhic Problems III, at 352-356; R. Simcha Krauss, The Sotheby's Case - A Halachic Perspective, IX Journal of Halacha & Contemporary Society 5, 10-13 (1985).

14. There is a dispute among Jewish law authorities as to whether such a transfer of title is effective if the original owner's ye'ush does not occur until after the transferee took possession.

15. See Shulhan Arukh, Hoshen Mishpat 356:1.

16. Id. The owner may try to recover from the thief, if he can find him, the amount the owner must pay to the buyer.

17. Id.

18. Id.

19. Id.

20. See, generally, J. David Bleich, Contemporary Halakhic Problems III, at 352.

21. Id.

22. Because the seller may have been somewhat averse to publicity - lest claimants learn about the art - the purchase price paid by the buyer may have been below market value.

23. Of course, in acquiring the property, such a bad faith purchaser would be guilty of violating the prohibition against buying stolen goods. See, e.g., Shulhan Arukh, Hoshen Mishpat 356:1.

24. Id.

25. J. David Bleich, Contemporary Halakhic Problems III, at 367; R. Yaakov Yeshaya Blau (contemporary), Pithei Hoshen IV, at 75.

26. Shulhan Arukh, Hoshen Mishpat 356:7; R. Yehiel Michel Epstein, Arukh ha-Shulhan, Hoshen Mishpat368:4.

27. Another example involves the doctrine of auto shel yam (literally, the "flooding of the sea"), whereby people acquire possession of property they save from imminent destruction. See, generally, J. David Bleich, Contemporary Halakhic Problems III, at 362-366.

28. See, generally, J. David Bleich, Contemporary Halakhic Problems III, at 356-362, 367-372.

29. R. Yaakov Yeshaya Blau (contemporary), Pithei Hoshen IV, at 79.

30. J. David Bleich, Contemporary Halakhic Problems III, at 355-356.

Courtesy of Jlaw.com

The Legal and the Mystical II

By Rabbi Eli Silberstein

The O.J. Simpson trial, which came to a sensational conclusion with a not-guilty verdict, made ever so clear the shortcomings of the American judicial system. In the face of compelling evidence pointing to his guilt, and his conviction in the subsequent civil suit, Mr. Simpson's acquittal reveals how legal procedure may actually interfere with the administration of justice. Had the jury, for instance, been given all the evidential information available to the judge, the verdict might have been quite different. But legal particulars forced the judge to withhold some of the evidence.

The Simpson case is not unique; it is rather reflective of a broader deficiency inherent in every legal system. Each system realizes a certain tension between legal requirements and justice in a fuller sense. Thus, in a particular case, all the proper rules and procedures may have been faithfully applied, but the judge may still experience doubt as to whether the outcome is in fact just.

These judicial discrepancies may lead the judge to assume that given the error-prone nature of human justice, it is safer, especially in cases involving capital punishment, to err in favor of the guilty, so as to avoid mistaken punishment of the innocent. Certainly, tensions between legal minutiae and moral sensibility are heightened when the conflict between the two is reversed and strict legal procedure dictates the execution of a defendant, while common sense justice advocates his exoneration, a theme that resonates poignantly in—among other literary works—Melville's *Billy Budd.*

Modern legal systems attempt to address these concerns by providing equity powers to judges in some cases, or by allowing appeals for executive clemency or pardon in others. Still, there often remains some nagging doubt as to whether true justice has been served.

We would be mistaken, however, to assume that this problem, inherent to most legal systems, is true of Jewish courts as well. For the procedures in an American court are not divinely ordained and are, in fact, in a perpetual process of revision and reinterpretation. So an American judge may readily acknowledge that the procedures of the moment may yield an improper result in a particular case. But in a Jewish court where the procedures do have divine authority, such resignation is entirely inappropriate. It is not for the judge to say whether basic procedures, such as the Torah law forbidding relatives from giving testimony, are effective in uncovering the truth; indeed, the notion that a given procedure is fallible is tantamount to blasphemy.

Consequently, the divine origin of Jewish law makes the tension between its precise execution and moral sensibilities largely irrelevant to the judge. Unlike other systems, the Jewish judge perceives the law to be perfect, and makes no allowances for occasional casualties of the system. He regards Jewish law as a perfect device in the procurement of justice, even when human sensibilities run against it. Thus, whenever there is a conflict, adherence to legal procedure will as a matter of principle, supersede human moral sensibilities.

The primacy of law over human reasoning is characteristic of the system in general. As an example, consider the law that regards a transaction fulfilled under gunpoint as valid, provided that the full market value had been paid for the property during the transaction. Jewish law claims that under such conditions, a seller ex post facto is considered to have genuinely consented to the sale. This is based on the presumption that a person would normally resign himself to a transaction when both his life is threatened if he refuses to sell and he receives full value for his property.

The obvious problem with this law is that it appears to distort justice by rewarding the criminal. Even if the extenuating conditions have indeed prompted the seller to fully consent to the sale, it still does not reflect the seller's true preferences; had the seller been given a choice, he would not have agreed to the sale. Yet Jewish law unambiguously applies the legal axiom which interprets consent to a sale as the relinquishment of ownership rights to the buyer.

Rabbi Loew (Maharal) discusses a similar issue with regard to a Talmudic law stating that if someone finds lost property, the object belongs to the finder if the original owner had, before the object was found, already despaired of ever recovering the property. This sense of despair (termed Yi'ush) is regarded as a form of formal relinquishment by the Talmud, and thus, the finder is free to take possession of the object. More strikingly, if a thief stole an object and sold it after the owner had despaired of recovery, the subsequent buyer is not required to return the stolen property. The thief is required to make restitution to the owner for the value of the object, but the owner no longer has any definitive claim to the object itself. While the finder, or present holder, may be encouraged to return the object, neither can be obligated to do so by the courts.

Many contemporaries of the Maharal criticized the Talmud because of this law. They were unhappy with the original owner losing claim to the property on the basis of regretful despair. Yet the Maharal defended this legal position, arguing that the law wisely must restrict itself to the hard facts surrounding the situation, rather than mandating a solution that appeals to intuitions of moral correctness.

The purpose of the law is to represent the objective truth about a given case. Jewish law regards ownership as more than a legal concept; the technical procedures by which property is transferred effect objective changes in the reality of ownership (see The Legal and the Mystical I, Wellsprings). In the case of duress then, the law can determine the status of the transaction only on the basis of the reality created when the seller consents to the transaction. Likewise, the status of a lost or stolen object is contingent on the owner's relationship to the object, without regard to extenuating circumstances: had the owner finally relinquished it? [Laws involving stipulation in a contract is another example for how Judaism perceives the power of transaction and ownership. See Tosaphot Ketubot 56a and Maimonides, Laws of Divorce, ch. Likutei Sichos vol. 6 and 19.]

Moral behavior, while encouraged in Judaism, is not enforced under the auspices of the law, but encouraged from outside its boundaries. Thus, while the Talmud clearly recommends that the finder return the object to the original owner, it does not mandate it. Justice, by its nature, is fundamentally descriptive, not prescriptive.

The law concerning sale under duress is an example of one case where the law does not respond to our own moral sensibilities, and yet it prevails. Other civil laws, however, go much further, altogether ignoring rational arguments.

For example, according to biblical law, if someone digs a pit in public property and an ox or a donkey falls into the pit, the digger is required to compensate the animal's owner for the damages caused by the pit. Reason would dictate that the same liability should apply if a person falls into that pit or if any valuable object is damaged by falling into the pit. Yet, Judaism's Oral Law infers from the biblical reference to an ox that a person is not eligible for restitution; similarly, the text's reference to a donkey implies the exclusion of liability for vessels.

Laws that are this arbitrary are the exception in Jewish civil law. However, their very existence has implications about the nature of the system as a whole. They reveal a mysterious side to the law and force us to take a more profound look at the meaning of law and justice in general.

On a most elemental level, justice is the fair and due treatment of economic or criminal situations which are at risk of going astray. In economic situations, it means securing property for those to whom it belongs. In criminal situations, it means punishing those who deserve to be punished. Of interest to us here is how Jewish law perceives civil disputes of ownership. These questions are of concern to any system of justice. But how are these questions resolved—who rightfully deserves the property or deserves the punishment and to what degree? In this regard, Judaism goes far beyond the conventional perception. Ownership or rights to ownership are not simply assigned to the person who happens to own an object, but rather to the one who is ultimately destined to own it.

Jewish mysticism explains that everything regarding a person's material possessions from the accumulation of property to the extent of a person's income or the manner in which he achieves that income, is preordained and suffused with divine meaning (See Legal and Mystical I). The law exists as an instrument which reveals and realizes the divine order. It serves in some mystical way as the blueprint of this preordained plan.

Rabbi Chaim ben Atar finds an allusion to this idea in the Biblical verse: "Do not cause perversion in the justice." The use of the definite article—"the justice"—suggests a pre-ordained plan. The judge's function is to act as an agent through whom this plan is implemented in each case. The laws in the Torah are a tool for achieving this pre-ordained result. If the judge fails to achieve this result, he denies justice on earth, and moreover, causes a perversion of divine order.

So the law is thus not merely a conduit to establish justice; it is justice itself. Human reasoning is important only insofar as it enables the judge to discern the law in a given case. In the words of Rabbi Soloveitchik: "Rabbinic scholars, when studying the Law, never ask 'why?' but rather 'what is the Law saying?'" This idea of justice is well illustrated by the procedures governing judicial decisions in capital cases.

A death sentence, according to Jewish law, may be imposed when a majority of judges support a guilty verdict regarding a capital crime. Oddly, however, the death sentence may not be carried out on a unanimous verdict. This derives from the principle that in a criminal case, the court must make every effort to find some grounds for protecting the defendant. Now if the judges are unanimous in their guilty verdict, the court will not succeed to find some way to argue in his defense.

Consider, then, a capital case where 22 out of 23 judges have voiced their opinion that the defendant is guilty. Suppose the last judge to express his opinion believes as well that the verdict should be that the accused is guilty. He knows that if he states this opinion openly, the defendant will be acquitted, in defiance of the court's perception of justice. He thus seems to face a moral quandary: Should he feign dissent from his colleagues' opinion so that the defendant receives the punishment he deserves? Or should he be honest about his position and so ensure a betrayal, as it were, of justice? The law requires the judge to express his opinion truthfully, notwithstanding the consequences thereof.

Suppose, on the other hand, that the last judge's opinion is at variance with the view of all the other judges. Now he faces the converse quandary. If he states his view honestly, he ensures that the defendant will be executed. Should he then say that he agrees with the other judges in order to save an innocent man from execution? Again, the law requires him to state his actual opinion, even if this obtains a result opposite of his intentions.

Both these positions illustrate the attitude of Jewish law to justice, as illustrated by the verse, "Do not respond to a grievance by yielding to the majority to pervert the law." A judge must recognize that his responsibility lies in pronouncing the law as he sees it, regardless of the outcome. If a judge yields to the majority in response to his personal convictions, he is actually perverting justice. Justice is defined by the law, and the judicial process is the vehicle for its realization. And the judge's role is to serve as facilitator.

It is upon this point that the distinction between Jewish and secular legal systems rests. For whereas even a secular system may, at least implicitly, concern itself with something beyond utilitarianism—indeed, in the Noachide Codes, the establishment of courts as dictated by human reason is divinely mandated, and often appeals to spiritual or philosophical ideals—it is uniquely the Jewish concept of justice that operates on a suprarational level. For only a divine system can reveal a reality as it ought to be, as it is informed by a higher perspective, and not constrained to the immediate reality of our own mortal perceptions.

At its most profound level, the realization of the divine order through the employment of justice, through doing justice, is what the Midrash refers to as the most divinely exalted virtue given by G-d as a gift to the Jewish nation. For it empowers us to transform the mundane world, and elevate it to a higher state. A judge who issues a just verdict, says the Talmud, is a "partner with G-d in creation." Taking the raw material of creation and imbuing it with G-dly meaning fulfills the divine intention in creation.

The idea that the Torah's legal system is of great esoteric significance is profoundly underscored by Rabbi Nissim of Girondi. Rabbi Nissim analyzes the words of criticism expressed by Samuel the prophet, in response to the Jewish people's request for a king who, in their own words, "will judge us like all the other nations." The Talmud states that Samuel would not have objected had they omitted from their plea the words "like all other nations" (as some of them evidently did). Samuel's disappointment was not simply a reaction to the people's desire for a monarchy in Israel. Monarchy may be perfectly legitimate, as the Torah itself instructs the Jewish people on how to appoint a king. More to the point, Samuel was dismayed by the manner of their request, as it betrayed obliviousness to the spiritual dimension of justice in which they, as Jews, had the privilege to participate.

Rabbi Schneur Zalman of Liadi explains that Torah study as an end in itself reflects the Law's spiritual nature. "A halacha," he states, "is the embodiment of the wisdom and the will of G-d, for it was His will that when, for example, Reuben pleads in one way and Simeon in another, the verdict as between them shall be thus and thus; and even should such a litigation never have occurred, nor ever presented itself for judgment in connection with such disputes and claims, nevertheless, it has been the will and wisdom of the Holy One, blessed be He, that in the event of a person pleading in this way, the verdict shall be such and such. Now therefore, when a person knows and comprehends with his intellect such a verdict in accordance with the law as it is set out in the Mishnah, Gemara or Poskim (codes), he has thus comprehended, grasped and encompassed with his intellect the will and wisdom of the Holy One, blessed be He, whom no thought can grasp, nor His will and wisdom, except when they are clothed in the laws that have been set out for us . . . This is a wonderful union, like which there is none other, and which has no parallel anywhere in the material world, whereby complete oneness and unity, from every side and angle, could be attained."

The view of the Midrash, that justice is primarily aimed at bringing the G-dly into the human realm, may help clarify the importance Judaism places on the human framework of justice. Having the divine permeate the human cannot mean the subordination of the human realm. On the contrary, it is by the full involvement of human intelligence in the revelation of the divine, that the dynamic unification of the G-dly and the human is manifested.

Rabbi Weinberg, the Chief Rabbi of Berlin in the 1920s, was asked by a Christian priest whether a Jewish court would accept his testimony. When the Rabbi responded in the negative, the priest asked whether a simple Jewish tailor would be eligible for testimony. Rabbi Weinberg answered that yes, Judaism does not distinguish between a great sage and a simple Jew with regard to his legal credibility in a court of law. The priest was deeply offended at the fact that he, a nobleman and leader of his faith, would have less weight before a Jewish court than the most illiterate Jews. Rabbi Weinberg then asked the priest whether he would be equally offended at the fact that he could not be counted as the tenth man for a minyan, despite the fact that an ordinary Jew would be counted without hesitation. The priest said that he was not bothered by that fact, as a prayer service was essentially a Jewish religious exercise, and thus was relevant only to members of the Jewish faith.

"For us Jews," said Rabbi Weinberg, "appearing before a Jewish court is a religious exercise as well."

Reprinted with permission from *Wellsprings Magazine*, a publication of Lubavitch Youth Organization

You Be The Judge

Lesson 3
When Glitter Turns Out To Be Gold

Introduction

In Guy de Maupassant's short story "The Necklace," a woman's life is financially ruined when she loses a borrowed diamond necklace and feels compelled to replace it. Only many years later does she discover that the necklace was in fact a fake. But what would happen if you lost some costume jewelry that you agreed to watch for a friend—and then discovered that the jewelry *was real?* How much would you be responsible to repay? This is the question we address in this lesson.

Bailment

The Difference between the Paid and the Unpaid Bailee

Learning Exercise

Text 1a

כִּי יִתֵּן אִישׁ אֶל רֵעֵהוּ כֶּסֶף אוֹ כֵלִים לִשְׁמֹר וְגֻנַּב מִבֵּית הָאִישׁ
אִם יִמָּצֵא הַגַּנָּב יְשַׁלֵּם שְׁנָיִם
אִם לֹא יִמָּצֵא הַגַּנָּב וְנִקְרַב בַּעַל הַבַּיִת אֶל הָאֱלֹהִים
אִם לֹא שָׁלַח יָדוֹ בִּמְלֶאכֶת רֵעֵהוּ

If one person gives another money or articles to watch, and they are stolen from the house of the person [keeping them], then if the thief is found, [the thief] must make [the usual] double restitution.

If the thief is not found, the owner of the house shall be brought to the courts, [where he must swear] that he did not lay a hand on his neighbor's property.

Shemot /Exodus 22:6-7

Text 1b

כִּי יִתֵּן אִישׁ אֶל רֵעֵהוּ חֲמוֹר אוֹ שׁוֹר אוֹ שֶׂה וְכָל בְּהֵמָה לִשְׁמֹר
וּמֵת אוֹ נִשְׁבַּר אוֹ נִשְׁבָּה אֵין רֹאֶה
שְׁבֻעַת ה׳ תִּהְיֶה בֵּין שְׁנֵיהֶם

אִם לֹא שָׁלַח יָדוֹ בִּמְלֶאכֶת רֵעֵהוּ וְלָקַח בְּעָלָיו וְלֹא יְשַׁלֵּם
וְאִם גָּנֹב יִגָּנֵב מֵעִמּוֹ יְשַׁלֵּם לִבְעָלָיו

If one person gives another a donkey, an ox, a sheep, or any other animal to watch, and it dies, is maimed, or is carried off in a raid, without eyewitnesses, then the case between the two must be decided on the basis of an oath to G-d.

If the [person keeping the animal] did not make use of the other's property, the owner must accept it [the oath, according to Rashi], and [the person keeping the animal] need not pay.

However, if it was stolen from [the keeper], then he must make restitution to [the animal's] owner.

Shemot 22:9-11

Working in pairs or small groups, answer the following three questions:

1. Both Text 1a and Text 1b open by providing examples of items given into custody.

What are the examples cited in 1a?

___

What are the examples cited in 1b?

___

2. Both Text 1a and Text 1b describe what happens in a case of theft.

Is the bailee liable for theft in the first case?

___

Is the bailee liable for theft in the second case?

3. Text 1b describes situations in which the bailee becomes exempt from liability by taking an oath of innocence. What do all these situations have in common?

4. Can you think of another example that might belong to this category of events?

You Be the Judge

One of the texts is referring to the laws of the paid custodian and one is referring to the laws of the unpaid custodian. Based on the differences you have noted in the text, identify which is which. How did you arrive at your conclusion?

Summary: The Responsibility of the Unpaid Bailee

3A. Comparison of Liability of Paid and Unpaid Bailees

	Unpaid Custodian	Paid Custodian
Responsible for Negligence		
Responsible for Theft		
Responsible for Act of G-d (unavoidable mishap)		

Applications

Can There Be Responsibility without Knowledge?

Case Study One: The Case of the Hidden Manuscript

Text 2

A person gave a friend a book to guard and the book was lost while under the supervision of the bailee, due to neglect. The owner claims that a rare manuscript, assessed at a thousand dollars, was tucked inside the book, and demands that the bailee give compensation for the value of the manuscript, in addition to the value of the book. The defendant does not question the owner's claim regarding the existence of the hidden manuscript, especially in light of some evidence that the owner presented, but claims to have had no knowledge of the existence of the manuscript when agreeing to be responsible for the care of the book.

Rabbi Yisrael Grossman, Responsa Netsach Yisrael (Jerusalem, 1986)

You Be the Judge

Is the bailee responsible for the value of the manuscript?

Text 3

חטין וחיפן בשעורין, שעורין וחיפן בחטין
אינו משלם אלא דמי שעורין בלבד

If a man gives his friend a bag of wheat and covers the top of the bag with barley, if the bag is lost or stolen, the bailee only pays for the value of a bag of barley.

Talmud, Bava Kama 62a

Question for Discussion

Based on the Talmudic statement quoted above, does your answer change?

Negligence vs. Active Damage

Case Study Two: The Case of the "Smoking Cash"

Text 4

A man gives the attendant in the public bath (*mikveh*) a bundle wrapped in newspaper to watch while he bathes. People frequently give the attendant their leavened bread before Passover to use as fuel in the furnace that heats the bath. The attendant forgets and throws the bundle he agreed to watch into the furnace with the other similar-looking packages. In fact, the bundle contained thousands of dollars in cash. The attendant had not been informed of the contents of the package.

From: Rabbi Yisrael Grossman, Responsa Netsach Yisrael (Jerusalem, 1986)

You Be the Judge

Does this case differ in any significant way from the previous case? Is the attendant obligated to repay the loss?

Text 5

אמר רבא: הנותן דינר זהב לאשה ואמר לה הזהרי בו של כסף הוא
הזיקתו, משלמת דינר זהב
משום דאמר לה: מאי הוה ליך גביה דאזקתיה
פשעה בו, משלמת של כסף
דאמרה ליה: נטירותא דכספא קבילי עלי, נטירותא דדהבא לא קבילי עלי

Rava said: If a man gave a woman a gold dinar for safekeeping, but told her that it was made of silver, and she damaged it [threw it in the sea, according to Rashi], then she must pay him a gold dinar, because he may say to her: "What right do you have to damage my property?" However, if she was merely negligent with it and lost it as a consequence, then she only has to pay him a silver dinar, for she may say to him: "The safekeeping of a silver dinar I accepted upon myself, but I did not accept upon myself the safekeeping of a gold dinar."

Talmud, Bava Kama 62a

Questions for Discussion

1. What is the key difference between these two cases in the Talmud?

2. In both cases, the woman is unaware of the value of the coin. Why is there greater liability in the first case?

3. Based on this reading in the Talmud, do you feel differently about how the second case should be decided?

Text 6

It would seem that the reason why the one who damages would have greater liability than one who is negligent is that in the case of damage, the person is actively causing the loss of the property, but in the case of negligence, there is no active involvement. That is why in the case of the gold dinar [where she was unaware of its value] she would be liable if she actively damages it, but not if she is merely negligent.

However, this is an incorrect assumption . . . Rather, the underlying reason for the distinction made in the Talmud between active damage and negligence has to do with the fact that the liability of negligence is predicated on the bailee's willingness to assume responsible for the loss of the deposit: [as Tosafot, *Ketubot* 56b explains the variant degrees of liability of different bailees (unpaid, paid, renter and borrower) are based on what the Torah assumes the bailee has committed himself to. These are not responsibilities that the Law imposes. The Law merely enforces that which the given bailee is assumed to have agreed to]. Therefore, the bailee cannot be held liable against his will for any responsibility he did not consent to.

Therefore, in the case where the woman was told the dinar was made of silver, she only accepted the liability of a silver dinar and she thus has no responsibility for the extra value that a gold dinar would have. [Even a borrower, for instance, would

Rabbi Aryeh Leib Heller (1745-1813), author of *Ketzot Hachoshen,* a commentary on Halachah. He served for a time as rabbi in Rozniatow, Ukraine (Galicia).

not be held liable for the extra value which he was not told about, as the borrower's liability is also predicated on his consent and commitment to the owner. He can only be held liable for what he committed himself to.] But in the case of negligence with fire, the Law imposes restitution obligations on the owner of the fire. The liability is not predicated on a voluntary commitment or consent.

Rabbi Aryeh Leib Heller, Ketzot Hachoshen 291:4

Question for Discussion

How does the view of the Ketzot affect the judgment in Rabbi Grossman's cases?

The Relevance of Intent in Cases of Damages

Text 7

אדם מועד לעולם בין שוגג בין מזיד בין ער בין ישן

A person is always liable, whether the damage was done intentionally or unintentionally, awake or asleep . . .

Talmud, Bava Kama 3b

Questions for Discussion

1. Based on Text 7, would the bath attendant's lack of evil intention be sufficient to absolve him of responsibility for payment?

2. Based on Text 8 below, are there any other extenuating circumstances in this case that make us think that the bath attendant should not be held liable for the full amount?

Text 8

המניח את הכד ברה”ר ובא אחר ונתקל בה ושברה, פטור
אמאי פטור? איבעי ליה לעיוני ומיזל . . .
לפי שאין דרכן של בני אדם להתבונן בדרכים

f someone places a pitcher in the middle of a public thoroughfare and a passerby stumbled on it and broke it, he is exempt from paying restitution . . . But why is he exempt, shouldn't he have looked where he was walking? [The reason is that] it is not the custom of pedestrians to look down at the roads.

Talmud, Bava Kama 27a-27b

An Object of Indeterminate Value (optional section)

Text 9

ראובן שאל משמעון סייף שהיה לו במשכון מעובד כוכבים ואבדו
ושואל ממנו ממון הרבה כמו ששואל ממנו העובד כוכבים
לא ישלם לו אלא דמי שוויו דסתם סייף דעלמא

Rabbi Yosef Caro of Safed (1488-1575), author of the *Shulchan Aruch,* "the Set Table," a compilation of Halachah recognized as authoritative by all Jewish communities. Born in Spain, he fled the Inquisition at the age of four with his family.

Reuven (Reuben) borrowed a sword from Shimon (Simeon) who had received the sword as collateral from a gentile neighbor for a limited period. Reuven lost the sword. Shimon claims the sword had unusual historical value according to the owner. He would have to reimburse the owner for its unique significance. The law says that Reuven owes compensation to Shimon for only an ordinary sword, because he was unaware of the special significance of the sword.

Rabbi Yosef Caro, Shulchan Aruch, Choshen Mishpat 72:8

Question for Discussion

According to Rabbi Yosef Caro, what would be the reason that the woman need only pay for a silver coin in the case where she is negligent?

Text 10

I am at a loss to understand the reasoning behind this law. For example, if someone would give a friend a precious stone to watch, and the stone got lost due to the friend's neglect, and the value of the stone had not been disclosed prior the agreement, could the friend possibly argue that he assumed the value to be far less? That would be preposterous! So why is the case of the sword different? It is true that in the Talmud in the case where the man gave a woman a coin of gold and told her it was made of silver, she is only responsible for the value of a silver coin, but that is because he deliberately misled her regarding the true value. Likewise, in the case where A gave B a bag of wheat and covered the top with barley, B is only responsible for the value of a bag of barley, for he intentionally disguised the contents of the bag.

Rabbi Shlomo Luria, Commentary on Talmud

Rabbi Shlomo Luria (the Maharshal) (1510-1574) of Posen. Best known for *Yam Shel Shlomo* (a halachic commentary) and *Chochmat Shlomo*, a commentary on the Talmud.

Question for Discussion

According to Rabbi Shlomo Luria, what is the reason that the woman is obligated to pay only the value of the silver coin in the case where she is negligent?

Text 11

In defense of the position of Rabbi Yosef Caro, I believe that the analogy that Rabbi Shlomo Luria made between the sword and a precious stone is erroneous, for it is common knowledge that a precious stone may have value that is not immediately apparent to the layman, and the assumption of responsibility to care for the stone implies that consent of the guardian to be liable for its true value.

Rabbi Shabtai Cohen (1621-1663), "the Shach," famous halachist who wrote *Siftei Kohen,* on the *Shulchan Aruch.*

Rabbi Shabtai Cohen (Shach), Commentary on Shulchan Aruch

Question for Discussion

According to Rabbi Shabtai Cohen, what is the reason that the Shulchan Aruch says the borrower is liable only for a regular sword?

The Legal and the Mystical

Layer upon Layer

Text 12

Our Sages tell us [that when a person's soul arrives in Heaven] if that person engaged in the study of Torah during its journey in the physical world, there is an announcement made "Fortunate is this soul who brought his study of Torah along with him." This means that the souls in Heaven study the same Torah as we study here on earth. So, for instance, when souls in Heaven study the Mishnah of "An ox which gored a cow to death and its calf was found dead next to it," their understanding of this law takes on a deeper spiritual level of meaning than the physical understanding that we have here on earth. Their understanding is removed from any physical phenomena . . . This is why the esoteric wisdom of the Torah is referred to as the soul of the Torah, while the actual physical law down here is referred to as the body of the Torah.

Rabbi Shne'ur Zalman of Liadi, Likutei Torah, Devarim/Deuteronomy 6:2

Rabbi Shne'ur Zalman of Liadi (1745-1813), "the Alter Rebbe," author of *Tanya,* an early classic of Chasidism, *Torah Or, Likutei Torah,* and *Shulchan Aruch HaRav,* a halachic commentary. Rabbi Shne'ur Zalman founded the Chabad school of mysticism.

Guarding a Sacred Trust

Text 13

וַיִּקַּח ה׳ אֱלֹקִים אֶת הָאָדָם וַיַּנִּחֵהוּ בְגַן עֵדֶן לְעָבְדָהּ וּלְשָׁמְרָהּ

And G-d took Adam and placed him in the Garden of Eden, to work it and to guard it.

Bereishit/Genesis 2:15

Learning Exercise

1. Some bailees watch objects primarily because they are providing a service for the owner, while other bailees watch objects as a consequence of receiving a service.

Sort the four major categories of bailees into two groups, Service Providers or Customers (those who are seeking a service).

3B. Guardians Sorted According to Service Orientation

Service Providers	Customers

Borrower Paid Bailee Renter Unpaid Bailee

2. Why did you choose to sort the four bailees in this way?

Key Points

1. A bailee is a person who has assumed responsibility for caring for another person's property.

2. The Torah discusses four prototypical bailee agreements: the unpaid custodian, the paid custodian, the renter, and the borrower.

3. An unpaid bailee is responsible for paying to compensate for loss or damage in the case of negligence but not in the case of unavoidable mishap.

4. Bailees can only be held accountable for responsibilities assumed at the time of the agreement.

5. People who damage other people's property must pay for the damage they cause even if they are unaware of the true cost of the damage.

6. Even those who cause damage should not be expected to foresee remote possibilities of damage.

7. The laws in the Torah have spiritual parallels.

8. We are placed in this world as guardians of a sacred trust.

Additional Readings

Whose Life Is It, Anyway?

Based on the teachings of the Lubavitcher Rebbe

By now everyone's heard the one about the guy who tells his buddy about the arrangement he and his wife arrived at after years of querulous marriage. "I decide the big issues," explains the triumphant husband, "and she decides the little things. World peace, the Economy, national politics—that's my department. She's in charge of the family budget, the kids' education, and the other everyday stuff . . . "

We often tend to think about our relationship with G-d along similar lines. When it comes to the minutiae of daily life, we basically decide things for ourselves. The big issues, on the other hand, that's G-d's department. The purpose of creation, the meaning of life—these are things that G-d has decided, and which we cannot hope to understand, much less influence in any way.

Chassidic teaching claims that the very opposite is the case.

When it comes to the do's and don'ts of daily living, the Torah presents us a very detailed list of instructions. Of course, we have free choice. But, on this level, "free choice" is not the authority to determine how things should be, to decide what's right and what's wrong. It means simply that we can choose to obey the divine will, thereby bringing our lives in harmony with the way that the creator of life designed it to be lived, or we can choose to disobey it. Since the latter choice is so obviously foolhardy and self-destructive, one is inclined to argue that it can hardly be considered a "free" choice at all! (On the other hand, it can be argued that this is the ultimate freedom—the freedom to act even against one's basic self-interest and intrinsic desire.)

In any case, the "little things" are G-d's call. But when it comes to the most basic questions of life, questions like, What are we? Why are we here?—here G-d says: "That's up to you. And whichever way you choose to define the raison d'être of your existence and your relationship with Me, that will become your truth. That is how I shall regard you and relate to you."

The Four Guardians

In one of his talks, the Lubavitcher Rebbe employs the model of the "Four Guardians," whose laws are laid down in this week's Parshah of Mishpatim (Exodus 21-24), to describe four types of human self-definition and the equivalent Divine response.

To understand the Rebbe's analysis (which is based on the writings of Rabbi Yeshayahu Horowitz, the great 16th century Torah scholar and Kabbalist known as "The Shaloh"), we first need to summarize the laws of the "Four Guardians," as set down in our Parshah and expounded in the Talmud and the Talmudic commentaries.

A "Guardian" (shomer) is any person who, for whatever reason, is responsible for an object belonging to another person. Altogether, the Torah classifies four types of Guardian and the level of responsibility to which each is held:

1) The Unpaid Guardian. The Unpaid Guardian is someone who is taking care of another's property purely as a favor and is receiving no compensation for his trouble. Although he is duty bound to care for the object, his responsibility in case of mishap is minimal. If the object is damaged or lost as a result of his negligence, he must pay; but as long as he has provided the reasonable care to which he had obligated himself, and takes an oath to that effect, he is absolved from responsibility.

2) The Paid Guardian. Since he is being paid (or otherwise compensated) for his services, the level of care he is expected to provide and his responsibility in the case of mishap is greater. Here the Torah differentiates between "avoidable damages," such as loss or theft, and "unavoidable damages" such as armed robbery and natural death. The Paid Guardian is responsible for the former and absolved by oath of the latter.

3). The Borrower. His is the highest level of liability. Unlike the first two guardians, whose care of the object is for the sake of its owner, the object has been given the borrower solely for his own benefit. As a result, he is responsible to return what has been given to him intact or else make good on its value—regardless of the degree of his fault in the case of damage. Even if the borrowed object is destroyed by a lightening bolt, the borrower must pay. [There are only two exceptions to the absolute responsibility of the Borrower: a) if the damage resulted from his normal use of the object; b) if the object's owner was with him at the time of the loss.]

4) The Renter. The Torah also mentions a fourth case in which a person is responsible for the property of his fellow, the case of the renter who pays for its use, but is unclear on the level of his responsibility. The Talmud cites two opinions on the status of the renter: Rabbi Judah rules that he is as the Unpaid Guardian, who is responsible only for outright negligence; Rabbi Meir

is of the opinion that his obligations are identical to those of the Paid Guardian, and he is liable also for "avoidable damages" such as loss and theft.

Why is the Renter a Fourth Category?

Obviously, these are not the only four cases in which a person has another person's object under his care. The scenarios leading to such a situation are virtually endless. But they all fall under one of the four categories. Indeed, the Talmud considers many other situations—i.e., a person who finds a lost object and is caring for it until the owner can be located, a person who is holding on to a fellow's object as collateral for a loan, etc. In each case the Talmud determines which of the four categories the said "guardian" belongs to.

This raises the question: Why, then, do we say that there are four Guardians? Why is the "Renter" regarded as a category unto itself, if the laws that govern a renter's culpability are identical either with those of an Unpaid Guardian (according to Rabbi Judah) or with those of a Paid Guardian (according to Rabbi Meir)?

The answer to this question lies in understanding the basis of the debate between Rabbi Judah and Rabbi Meir regarding the status of the Renter.

A person who rents an object receives the object in order to derive use from it, and pays the owner for this privilege. According to Rabbi Judah, the payment offered by the renter is in return for, and of equivalent value to, the right of use he enjoys. Therefore, the fact that he benefits from the possession of his fellow's property, and the fact that the owner is paid, should have no bearing on the level of his responsibility—they cancel each other out. This means, says Rabbi Judah, that the renter receives nothing in return for the care he is providing for the object. Hence his status as an Unpaid Guardian.

Rabbi Meir does not disagree with the above tally of privileges and liabilities. But he has a completely different perspective on the "Renter." According to Rabbi Meir, the primary issue should be not how much a Guardian receives in return for his trouble, but why it is in his possession in the first place. The question of payment or non-payment is secondary. In the case of both the Paid Guardian and the Unpaid Guardian, the object has entered their domain for the sake of the owner. So the responsibility is minimal. In the case of the Unpaid Guardian it is limited to outright negligence; in the case of the Paid Guardian, the fact that there is also some benefit for the Guardian means that the level of responsibility is to be raised a notch.

But in the case of the Borrower and the Renter, says Rabbi Meir, the opposite is true: the object has left its owner's control for the sake of the Guardian. So the responsibility is total. The addition of the other, secondary factor, that of payment, has a similar effect as in the case of the Paid Guardian: because the renter pays for the favor, his level of responsibility is lowered a notch. As Rabbi Meir sees it, the Paid Guardian is basically an Unpaid Guardian who has been paid to be slightly more responsible, while the Renter is basically a Borrower who has paid to reduce his responsibility. The fact that the technical result is that the Renter and the Paid Guardian are culpable for the same set of circumstances is entirely incidental. In essence, the Paid Guardian has more in common with the Unpaid Guardian, and the Renter has more in common with the Borrower, than the two have in common with each other.

In the words of the Talmud, according to Rabbi Meir, "There are Four Guardians, though their laws are three." Indeed, the classification of "Four Guardians" is attributed solely to Rabbi Meir. According to Rabbi Judah, there are, indeed, only three "Guardians," the renter being a form of Unpaid Guardian.

On the Spiritual Plane

All of the above also applies to the inner life of the soul and its relationship with its Creator.

Man's role in creation is that of a Guardian. "And G-d took the man and placed him in the Garden of Eden, to work it and to keep it" (Genesis 2:15). The Creator entrusted His world to our care, charging us with the responsibility of safeguarding and developing the resources and potentials which He has granted and made available to each individual.

The Torah's laws of guardianship address some of life's most central questions. Whose life is it, anyway? Do we possess an inherent right to "life, liberty, and the pursuit of happiness" or must we earn these rights? What are our responsibilities towards our Creator and the rewards we might anticipate in reciprocation, and what is the correlation between these responsibilities and rewards? Is it enough to "do our best" and expect life's blessings to flow to us, or is reward measured by achievement?

The "Four Guardians" (using Rabbi Meir's model) represent four approaches to life. The first is the altruistic "Unpaid Guardian," the individual who exemplifies the ideal "I was not created, but to serve my Creator" (Talmud, Kiddushin 82b). The Unpaid Guardian sees his life, his talents and his possessions as Divine property which has been placed in his trust "to work and to keep." Nor does he feel that G-d owes him anything in compensation for his efforts.

On the other extreme is the "Borrower," who believes that all that he has been given has been given for his own benefit. To the Borrower, the purpose of life is self-fulfillment and self-realization. He may acknowledge who the ultimate Owner is and accept his obligations toward Him as a Guardian (to the extent that he fulfills, to the letter, every dictate of Torah law); but he does not feel that he owes anyone anything for the use of life's blessings.

The "Paid Guardian" and the "Renter" occupy the middle ground between these two extremes. On the issue of "Why are we here?" they differ as much as do the Unpaid Guardian and the Borrower; but they each temper their perspective on life with the idea of "payment." The spiritual Renter is a Borrower in that he sees the purpose of it all as the fulfillment and enhancement of self, but nevertheless feels that he ought to earn this privilege by "also" serving his Creator. The Paid Guardian is like the Unpaid Guardian in that he sees the fulfillment of G-d's will as the ultimate purpose of life; he differs only in that he reserves for himself a small corner of self-interest. He feels that he also deserves something of "a life of his own" in return for his work as a Guardian in the employ of the Almighty.

Which is it Really? All of Them

Our sages tell us that G-d deals with us "measure for measure," responding to us in the manner in which we behave and define our relationship with Him. Thus Rabbi Israel Baal Shem Tov interprets the verse "G-d is your shadow" (Psalms 121:5)—the Almighty allows us to establish the basis and tone of our relationship with Him and responds in kind, just as a person's shadow moves in concert with the person's movements.

Man has been given free reign in choosing the mode of "guardianship" to define his life. Man may choose the "free lunch" approach of the Borrower. But then, says the Almighty, you must take full responsibility, as well. If things go awry in your life, if you err and blunder, or even if circumstances beyond your control overwhelm you—that's your problem. After all, it was you who decided that it's "your" life.

Or, a person may assume a Renter's self-definition, in which case he is relieved of some of the "responsibility." Because he senses his indebtedness to the Creator, he need not bear the burdens of life on his own. The same is true of the Paid Guardian. True, he has not given himself over entirely to his guardianship, reserving his "right" for reward, but his basic approach to life is that it is not his but his Creator's. Responding "measure for measure," the Almighty relates to him in a similar fashion: the "laws" which govern his life protect him, to a certain extent, from an utter abandonment to "fate," but leave him somewhat exposed to the uncertainties and mishaps which threaten our pitfall-prone existence.

But the Unpaid Guardian is absolved from vulnerability to everything save outright negligence. As long as he remains faithful to his mission in life, he need not be worried by the trappings of the material world. Because he has relinquished all vestiges of self, because he sees his life solely in terms of his service of his Creator, G-d takes full responsibility for his life.

Four Excuses

By Yanki Tauber

The "That's how G-d made me" excuse:

Why shouldn't I do whatever I want? After all, if I want it, that means that there's something inside me telling me to want it, right? I'm just being me. Isn't it natural for me to be me?

The "Sorry, I lost it" excuse:

Look, I know it's wrong. But I can't control myself. I have this violent streak in me that . . . well, once you start me off, I can't stop.

The "I'm special" excuse:

I'm an artist/business tycoon/holy man//commander-in-chief/heiress/scientist. I have very special talents and abilities and great things to accomplish. The regular rules don't apply to me. I can't be constrained by laws designed to keep the herd in line.

The "Little me" and "What's the use" excuse

You know, I used to care about these things and try to right the world's wrongs. But what's the point? The world is what it is, and what I do or don't do won't make much difference anyway. I just let things be. Relax, let things take their course.

The Torah reading of Mishpatim ("Laws"—Exodus 21-24) includes much of what can be called the Torah's "civil code"—the laws governing criminal assault, theft, damages, loans and rentals, employer-employee relations, etc. But as the Chassidic masters repeatedly remind us, everything in Torah has both a "body" and a "soul": the most lofty or esoteric concept has a practical application, and the most technical law has a spiritual import.

Mishpatim includes the laws of the Four Prototypes of Damages (as the Talmud defines them) —"the animal, the pit, the man and the fire." Technically, these describe four basic categories of damages for which a person is responsible: 1) "Animal": damage caused by one's animal or other possession (e.g., your ox gores your neighbor's cow; your goat eats up your neighbor's tomato plants); 2) "Pit": passive damage caused by one's criminal negligence (e.g., you dig a hole in the middle of the street and someone falls in and breaks a leg); 3) "Man": active, human-inflicted damages (e.g., you break his $1000 lamp or the only nose on his face); 4) "Fire": damages arising from the failure to control potentially damaging forces that are one's responsibility to control (e.g., you're burning garbage in your back yard and it spreads to your neighbor's property).

The "Four Prototypes of Damages," says the Lubavitcher Rebbe, also describe four spiritually damaging phenomena: the tendency to blindly and indiscriminately follow our wiles and desires ("the animal"); the failure to control anger and other destructive forces in our psyche ("fire"); the delusion that everything is permitted in pursuit of a "higher" goal ("man"); and the inertia of the passive, hollowed-out soul ("the pit").

As the laws of Mishpatim warn against and prescribe the remedies for the physical "Prototypes of Damages," so does the "soul of Torah" counteract its four spiritual analogs:

Yes, our animal instincts are natural, necessary and desirable; but only when guided and directed by the higher instincts of our G-dly soul.

Yes, volatile forces rage within us; but we have been given the responsibility, and the means, to control them.

No, our highest and most spiritual aspirations are not exempt from the rule of law. On the contrary, when they fail to submit to its higher authority, they become the cause for the greatest evils perpetuated by man.

Indeed, passivity is all too easy a rut to roll into. We must constantly remind ourselves that our actions do make a difference in G-d's world: He created it, He entrusted us with the task to improve it, and He supplied us the resources to do so. We need only scratch the surface of our soul to uncover the faith, the will, the passion and the energy to act.

You Be The Judge

Lesson 4
The Parasite

Introduction

Your son (a poor starving college student) is backpacking with friends across America this summer, so you decide to give him a cell phone. When he comes back, he tells you how he earned $2,000 renting out the cell phone to friends. Well, of course you are quite proud of your young entrepreneur, and thank him for giving you such a great return on your investment.

Except it turns out your son has no intention of handing the money over to you. If pushed to the wall, he will perhaps agree to reimburse you for the cost of the phone and the service charge, but he thinks the profits should be his.

Now your young entrepreneur is starting to look like a little opportunist, so you take the case to your local rabbi. It turns out that Jewish scholars have spent quite some time debating this sort of question.

Their discussion is the subject of today's class.

Doing Business Using Someone Else's Cow
Responsibilities of Borrowers and Renters

4A. Comparison of Liability of Paid and Unpaid Bailees

	Unpaid Bailee	Paid Bailee
Responsible for Negligence		
Responsible for Theft		
Responsible for Act of G-d (unavoidable mishap)		

4B. Summary of Circumstances Under Which Bailees Are Liable

	Unpaid Bailee	Paid Bailee	Renter	Borrower
Negligence				
Theft				
Unavoidable mishap				

Can a Renter Profit from the Loss of the Rental?

Text 1

השוכר פרה מחבירו והשאילה לאחר ומתה כדרכה
ישבע השוכר שמתה כדרכה והשואל ישלם לשוכר
אמר רבי יוסי: כיצד הלה עושה סחורה בפרתו של חבירו?אלא תחזור פרה לבעלים

If someone hires a cow from another person and then lends it to someone else, and the animal dies naturally while in the borrower's care, the hirer of the cow must take an oath before the owner to affirm that it died naturally [since a hirer is not liable if the animal died or was harmed by forces beyond his control], and the borrower must pay the hirer the value of the cow [since a borrower is liable even if the borrowed thing died or was damaged by accident, and the borrower must reimburse the person from whom he borrowed it].

Rabbi Yosi [disagreed with this opinion and] said: How can the hirer do business using another person's cow [and make a profit from it]? [If the first opinion is correct, a very strange situation is being created whereby the owner of the cow receives no compensation for its loss, and the hirer, who does not own it and whose right to its use is limited, receives full compensation for its loss!] Rather, [says Rabbi Yosi, the owner is allowed to deal directly with the borrower:] the borrower [does not reimburse the hirer, but] must return the value of the cow directly to its owner.

Talmud, Bava Metsia 35b

You Be the Judge

Do you think the renter should be allowed to keep the money?

Applications

Case Study One: The Case of the Frequent Flyer

Rabbi Shmuel Vozner (1913-), born in Vienna, studied at the Chachmei Lublin yeshiva in Lublin. Immigrated to Israel before WWII. Author of many works on Jewish law, including *Shevet HaLevi* ("The Tribe of Levi").

Text 2

You travel a lot for a company at the company's expense. Due to your frequent flyer status, you are eligible for a free ticket in return for the mileage accrued.

Rabbi Shmuel Vozner, Shevet HaLevi, vol. 9, no. 305

You Be the Judge

Can you use the free ticket, or does the free ticket belong to the company for which you work?

Case Study Two: The Case of the Tenant Who Bought Insurance

Text 3

A tenant realized that the house he lived in was not insured. He decided to take out insurance on his landlord's property. A year later the house burned down. The insurance company paid the tenant for the loss of the house. The landlord is now suing the tenant for this money, arguing that since he is the owner of the property he is entitled to the money. The question is: Does the axiom "one cannot do business with another's property" apply here? Or perhaps this is entirely different. Since the tenant invested money in the insurance policy, shall we consider him to be doing business with his *own* money?

Case recorded by Rabbi Meir Simcha Cohen of Dvinsk
Or Same'ach, Laws of Hiring 5:6

Rabbi Meir Simcha Cohen of Dvinsk (1843-1926), recognized as an extraordinary scholar at an early age. Rabbi of Dvinsk from 1887 until his death. Author of *Or Same'ach*, a commentary on Rambam, and *Meshech Chochmah* ("Price of Wisdom").

You Be the Judge

Should the tenant be allowed to keep the insurance money, or must it be handed over to the landlord?

Question for Discussion

In what way is the rental fee unlike the insurance premium?

Case Study Three: The Case of the Warehoused Library

Text 4

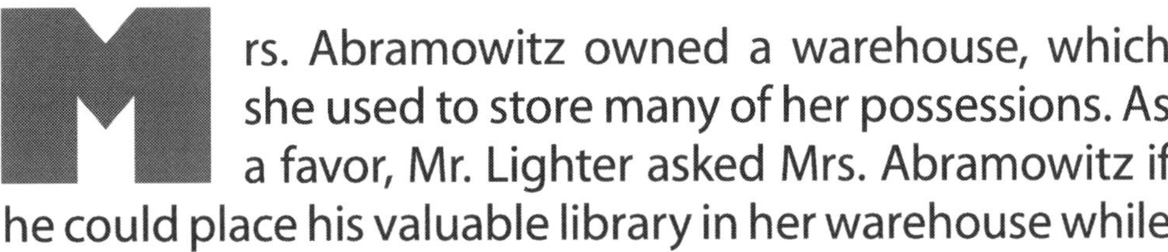

Mrs. Abramowitz owned a warehouse, which she used to store many of her possessions. As a favor, Mr. Lighter asked Mrs. Abramowitz if he could place his valuable library in her warehouse while he was away, so that it would be protected from theft or damage. Mrs. Abramowitz agreed to do so without asking for any pay. While Mr. Lighter was away, a fire broke out in the warehouse, and many of its contents, including Mr. Lighter's library, were totally destroyed. Mrs. Abramowitz had insurance on the warehouse and its contents. The question before the court is whether: a) Mrs. Abramowitz can make an insurance claim for the library which she did not own, and b) if she is entitled to the money for the library, can Mr. Lighter request some or all of the money paid to her for the library's value?

Rabbi Ezra Batzri in Techumin 2:449

Rabbi Ezra Batzri is a contemporary legal scholar, who has served on the Jerusalem Rabbinical High Court.

Learning Exercise

You are a lawyer defending Mrs. Rabinowitz before a beit din. Craft an argument that shows that there is a logical distinction between Rabbi Yosi's case of the renter doing business using someone else's cow and Mrs. Rabinowitz's case.

NOTES

Mishnah	Abramowitz

4C. Distinctions between Mishnah and Abramowitz Cases

	Mishnah	Abramowitz
Or Same'ach	When cow is hired, the hirer does not anticipate the renter profiting from the hire	When insurance is bought, the insurer anticipates the possibility of the insured profiting from the purchase of insurance
Mahari Halevi	Renter is physically using cow for profit by renting it out	Mrs. Abramowitz is not using Mr. Lighter's property for profit, but independently paying insurance
Maharash Engel, Machaneh Efraim	Borrower pays to compensate for the loss of the cow, so payment has to go to the person who sustained the loss	Insurance company is paying according to terms of the agreement to insured, and not to compensate for an unanticipated loss

Moore v. UCLA

Text 5

אין לאדם רשות על גופו כלל

person has no [ownership] rights at all when it comes to his body.

Rabbi Shne'ur Zalman of Liadi, Shulchan Aruch, Choshen Mishpat, Hilchot Nizkei Guf Ve'nefesh (Laws of Damages of Body and Soul), no. 4

The Legal and the Mystical

Text 6a

לְדָוִד מִזְמוֹר לַה׳ הָאָרֶץ וּמְלוֹאָהּ תֵּבֵל וְיֹשְׁבֵי בָהּ

he earth, and all that fills it, belongs to HaShem.

Tehillim/Psalms 24:1

Text 6b

לִי הַכֶּסֶף וְלִי הַזָּהָב נְאֻם ה׳ צְבָאוֹ–ת

he silver and gold are Mine, says HaShem.

Chagai/Haggai 2:8

Text 7

From a divine perspective, there is no difference between human life and other physical property, as the entire world is equally G-d's. However, there is a difference between the two in the world of human experience. Body and soul are delivered to the person in a way whereby one can openly witness the divine ownership of them, as we say each day: "The soul which You gave me [anew every single day]." The divine mandate that the human being is charged with in performing the divine laws of the Torah further exhibits the divine nature of human life.

Rabbi Menachem Mendel Schneerson (The Lubavitcher Rebbe)
Likutei Sichot, vol. 34, p. 109

Rabbi Menachem Mendel Schneerson (1902-1994), also known simply as "the Rebbe." Born in southern Ukraine. Rabbi Schneerson escaped from the Nazis, arriving in the U.S. in June 1941. The Rebbe emphasized the importance of traditional Jewish teachings concerning Mashiach, often reminding people that the performance of just one additional good deed could usher in the era of Mashiach.

Key Points

1. People engaged in economic activity sometimes find an opportunity to make profits using someone else's property. This situation is referred to in the Talmud as "doing business using someone else's cow."

2. In the classic case of "doing business using someone else's cow," a man hires a cow, lends it to a borrower, and then attempts to recover the cost of the dead cow from the borrower (who is obligated to pay for unavoidable death) even though renters do not need to repay owners for the unexpected death of an animal. The Talmud requires the renter to give the money to the original owner.

3. When frequent flyer miles accrue in an employee's name from business travel tickets paid for by the employer, a situation similar to the classic case is created, and according to Talmudic law, the employer would have the right to the frequent flyer miles.

4. When the renter of a property insures that property (although the owner did not), a situation similar to the classic case is created. The purchase of insurance may differ from the classic case, however, because the renter is investing his own resources, and also because, when the insurance is purchased, there is an explicit expectation that the person paying the premium will reap the benefits in the event of mishap.

5. In cases where the law is unclear, a beit din prefers to negotiate a compromise in which the disputed sum is apportioned so that the person faced with the greater loss receives two thirds, and the other party receives one third.

6. In order to rule in a particular case, a beit din often must concern itself with determining the prior expectations of the parties.

7. When a doctor uses genetic material from a patient (cells, blood, etc.) to develop commercially valuable products, a situation similar to the classic case is created. The situation differs, however, in that according to Jewish law, we are not owners of our own bodies.

Additional Reading

A Special Report: WHO OWNS YOUR GENES?

By Gina Kolata

Erich Karl Fuchs had his first AIDS test in 1988. The test, he thought, would confirm the inevitable—it would show he was infected with the AIDS virus. Mr. Fuchs, who is gay, had had unprotected sex over the years with men who carried the virus. It stood to reason that he, too, would be infected. But, to his astonishment, the test showed no evidence of the virus. "I said, 'This has got to be wrong,'" Mr. Fuchs said. "Then I took the test again and I took it again." The results never varied.

Over the next six years, Mr. Fuchs repeatedly got in touch with AIDS researchers and asked them to study him and figure out why he seemed to be immune to the virus, H.I.V. But, he said, the scientists told him they were not interested. Finally, in 1994, Mr. Fuchs, still uninfected, tried again at a place he had approached earlier, the Aaron Diamond AIDS Research Center in New York. This time, he said, the researchers agreed to study him. The result was dumbfounding. Try as they might, in laboratory tests, the center's scientists could not get the AIDS virus to enter Mr. Fuchs's cells.

After months of fevered research, the scientists at Aaron Diamond discovered why Mr. Fuchs and another man with a similar experience were immune. The men had inherited a gene that results in a blocked porthole into white blood cells, preventing the virus from slipping in. The investigators went on to isolate the gene, discover how it worked and learn how many other people have it. On May 2, the research center was awarded a patent for a test to identify people who have the H.I.V.-resistance gene, allowing it to share in any profits from the test. But what about Mr. Fuchs and the other man, Steve Crohn? They say they approached Aaron Diamond scientists and suggested that they be studied. They offered their blood, they participated in the research project, they helped the research center garner publicity for its discovery. "I just wanted to do something good," Mr. Fuchs said. "But once money came into the picture, why not have it be shared with me?"

These days more and more patients are asking the same question. Laboratories offer tests for more than 700 human genes, with more being discovered almost daily. And, for almost every gene, some medical institution or some company owns a patent on its use.

"The value of patients' tissues has potentially gone up enormously," said Dr. Barry Eisenstein, the vice president for science and technology at the Beth Israel Deaconess Medical Center in Boston. But, Dr. Eisenstein said, patients whose cells provided the genes that have been patented are almost never compensated.

Whether any money has been made from tests based on their genes—and in the case of the AIDS-resistance gene, none yet has—some patients have become wary about providing their tissue for genetic research. A few have demanded money up front before providing tissue. Others are writing contracts spelling out what they are entitled to if they help scientists find genes. Some experts on patent law say that it would be unfortunate if patients start demanding financial rewards for participating in research.

"I hate to create incentives that would lead people to get greedy," said Rebecca Eisenberg, a patent law expert at the University of Michigan. "I am worried that there are just too many mouths at the feeding troughs of pharmaceutical products." Other experts say the current system of awarding gene patents seems unjust.

Dr. Robert Cook-Deegan, an investigator at the Kennedy Institute of Ethics at Georgetown University, said: "We have a system where the research participants are treated as pure altruists, but everyone else is treated as a pure capitalist. I don't think that's quite fair." The problem, said Hank Greely, a law professor at Stanford University, is that the rules of the game seem to have changed.

"It used to be that when you were a research subject, you were doing it for free and you assumed that the people on the other side were doing it for free—at least for academic research," Professor Greely said. "These days, there is very little academic research that doesn't have some commercial interest, and almost always now the researcher has a potential commercial interest. Someone might say, 'Look, I'm willing to do this for the good of humanity if everyone else is, too. But if someone on the other side is going to make billions of dollars, I want some, too.'"

The Families I: Searching for the Good from Sorrow

Daniel M. Greenberg, a real-estate lawyer in Homewood, Ill., never thought about potential profit when he helped get a gene search going. All he wanted was to help other families avoid what had happened to him and his wife.

The Greenbergs' first child, Jonathan, was born on June 12, 1981, a perfect present for their fourth anniversary. But they soon began to worry. Jonathan did not roll over when he was supposed to. He never sat up. Finally, when Jonathan was a year old, a neurologist discovered that he had Canavan disease, a rare genetic disorder that is invariably fatal and almost exclusively strikes Ashkenazi Jews, those who trace their origins to Eastern and Central Europe.

The Greenbergs were told that Jonathan's condition would only get worse and that he would die before he was a teenager. (He died when he was 11 years old.)

"Obviously, our lives were shattered," Mr. Greenberg said. "It was a tough haul trying to think of your child as a dying child and never being able to do the things that other children can do."

Then the Greenbergs' second child, Amy, turned out to have the disease, too. Desolate, Mr. Greenberg eventually decided that maybe something good could come out of his tragedy if he could help scientists find the gene that, when mutated, leads to Canavan disease. In 1987, he found a researcher who was eager to do the work, Dr. Reuben Matalon at the University of Illinois Hospital in Chicago. Mr. Greenberg said he organized tens of thousands of dollars in donations and grants for the project, including several thousand dollars of his own money, and helped Dr. Matalon obtain needed blood, urine and skin biopsy samples from children with Canavan disease and their parents.

Dr. Matalon began making progress. Then he was recruited by Miami Children's Hospital, which wanted him to establish a center for research on genetic diseases, with a multimillion-dollar annual budget. At the University of Illinois Hospital, Dr. Matalon said, his research budget, excluding donations, had been no more than $10,000 a year. It was in Miami, with substantial financing from Children's Hospital, that Dr. Matalon, in 1993, finally isolated the Canavan disease gene. "My contract said every invention I make would be theirs, and that's it," Dr. Matalon said. "I am not in the inventing business. I am a research person. If they make money on me, I don't care."

The patent for the gene was issued to the Miami Children's Hospital Research Institute on Oct. 21, 1997. In the meantime, Dr. Matalon had moved on to the University of Texas Medical Branch at Galveston. The Miami Children's Hospital Research Institute, an affiliate of the hospital, retains control of the commercial uses of the Canavan disease gene.

Marc Golden of Golden Group Intellectual Capital was brought in to help the hospital decide how best to use the patent. At first, he said, the hospital considered donating the gene patent to the public and forgoing royalties on any test. It eventually chose not to, he said, because it feared that there were so few people who needed the test that laboratories would not bother to publicize it.

After months of deliberations and negotiations with academic and commercial laboratories, Mr. Golden said, the hospital decided to charge a royalty fee of $12.50 per test. The money, he said, would partly offset the hospital's costs in paying for Dr. Matalon's research, and the amount would not be overly burdensome to people paying for the test. The hospital hopes to use some of the royalty money to publicize the test, he added. But the families who got the research going are not assuaged. They want the gene test in the public domain, available to laboratories free of charge and free of the encumbrance of licensing agreements.

"We gave our samples to be used for the public good," said Judith Tsipis, a parent of a boy with Canavan disease and the director of the genetic counseling program at Brandeis University. "They were not given to Miami Children's. Had they told us they wanted to patent it, we probably would have found another researcher who had the same goals as we did. Finding the gene is not an impossible task."

Mr. Greenberg shares her sentiments. "I am disappointed and disheartened and disgusted," he said.

The Families II: Aiding Research, with a Wider View

Like Daniel Greenberg, Sharon Terry of Sharon, Mass., found herself with two children with a rare genetic disease that she had never known existed. And like Mr. Greenberg, Ms. Terry realized that the only way anyone would look for the gene that made her two children ill would be if she provided money, body tissue and medical histories from families whose members harbored the gene. But Ms. Terry did one thing that had never occurred to Mr. Greenberg. She and her husband, Patrick, made researchers sign a contract giving the families rights to share in the profits from any gene patent that might arise.

Ms. Terry's son and daughter have pseudoxanthoma elasticum, which causes mineralization of elastic tissue. The most serious consequence is blindness, which occurs when the membrane behind the retina calcifies and develops cracks. Blood vessels leak through the cracks, destroying vision. "There were people dabbling in the disease, but their major frustration was that they had just four or five families," Ms. Terry said. She saw an opportunity. Establishing a foundation, PX International, Ms. Terry and her husband, a manager of a construction company, found 2,000 people with the disease, set up a repository to store tissue samples, and began raising money for research. It took them just four years.

"We said, 'We can get you as many sibling pairs and as many patients as you want,' " Ms. Terry said she told researchers. The group had no trouble finding scientists who were eager to work with them. "They are so delighted that we will do all the grunt work," she said.

The researchers happily signed her group's agreement, Ms. Terry said. They readily agreed to its clause saying that the foundation had to be named in any patent applications arising from the work, that any profits or revenue from the discoveries be shared with the foundation and that any genetic test must be made readily available to the foundation, she said. Now, Ms. Terry said, the gene has been found. She worked closely with the Genetic Alliance, an advocacy group in Washington for people with genetic diseases, in formulating the contract.

"More and more of our organizations are interested in this, and they become savvy very fast," said Mary Davidson, the alliance's executive director. The groups are familiar with the Canavan disease story and they have taken careful note, Ms. Davidson said.

But there can be a danger in demanding too much too soon. "People may find that if they overreach in these contracts, the thing that they felt so valuable is something no one is interested in pursuing," said Robert P. Merges, a law professor specializing in patent law at the University of California at Berkeley.

That happened to a Boston family whose members had long life spans, which made them of great interest to Dr. Thomas Perls, a gerontologist at the Beth Israel Deaconess Medical Center in Boston. The family told Dr. Perls that he could use their tissue to search for a longevity gene, but only if the medical center paid a huge sum of money. Dr. Perls refused.

Dr. Eisenstein, of Beth Israel Deaconess, said the medical center was uncomfortable with paying one family when others were donating their tissue. But, he said, there are no rules in this new arena, and the hospital might well have reached a different decision if a group of long-lived families had formed an organization like PX International. "The bottom line is that none of us are smart enough to know where to begin," Dr. Eisenstein said. "There is no easy answer. We're in the midst of a national debate."

The Future: Searching for Fair Treatment of All

Mr. Crohn and Mr. Fuchs, the men who are resistant to the AIDS virus, would like to press their claims. "Somebody, somewhere, has to decide who owns our genetic material," Mr. Crohn said. But, the men said, it is beyond their means to take on this legal battle. They take comfort in the fact that two of the scientists they dealt with at Aaron Diamond, both of whom have since moved to other institutions, said they personally would be pleased if the two men could receive some compensation, assuming the patent ever makes money.

But David Jackson, a lawyer in Hackensack, N.J., whose firm filed for the patent on behalf of the Aaron Diamond AIDS Research Center, said the question of whether to compensate Mr. Crohn and Mr. Fuchs never came up as part of the process of obtaining the patent. And experts in patent law say that in the few cases like this that have gone to court, the outcomes favored the patent holders and not the individuals who asked for a share of patents.

The most famous legal case over ownership of tissue involved John Moore, a man with a rare form of leukemia who argued that researchers in California took his cells, realized the cells made a valuable biological substance, and patented cell cultures derived from his body. Mr. Moore sued, asserting that the cells were his property and demanding their return. But in 1990 the California Supreme Court ruled that he and other patients did not have property rights over their tissue.

Then there was the case of Marlo Brown of Petaluma, Calif. In the early 1980s, Ms. Brown noticed that several cats in an animal shelter that she ran were ill with a disease that looked to her like AIDS. She took the cats and detailed notes to an animal virologist at the University of California at Davis and suggested that they had a feline version of AIDS and that he use their tissue to find the virus.

He did, and ended up discovering not only a feline AIDS virus but also a test for it and a vaccine to protect cats. The University of California obtained patents on the test and the vaccine. But Ms. Brown asked what about her? Was she not an inventor too? A Federal District Court said in the mid-1990s that she was not, ruling that her contribution did not entitle her to share in the patent.

Professor Eisenberg, the patent expert from the University of Michigan, said the courts say that patents for molecules like genes should go to the person who envisions what they look like and identifies a practical use for them. "You can't envision a molecule by saying, 'Here's a disease, here's some tissue, go for it,' " she said. "The fact is that we rely on the private sector to develop diagnostic and therapeutic products, and the private sector is profit driven," Professor Eisenberg said.

"People may contribute their tissue in the expectation that nobody is going to make a profit on it, but that's a little naïve. There's no free lunch here."

The reason for patents is to provide incentives for inventors, Professor Eisenberg said. "When people see these innovations creating millionaires and billionaires overnight," she said, "they may think, 'Why not me?' " But, she said, the truth is somewhat different. "Most patents have no value," Professor Eisenberg said. Developing gene products, she said, "is a very risky invention—you have an occasional big winner that justifies all the dry holes."

But, said Professor Merges, the patent expert at the University of California at Berkeley, scientists should not be surprised when patients feel cheated. "It would be hypocritical for a researcher to say, 'I'm outraged that patients are interested in the commercialization of their tissue' while at the same time the researcher has his name on fifteen patents," Professor Merges said. "There's a sort of mercantilization going on in medicine."

The risk, said Professor Greely of Stanford, is that patients will refuse to participate in genetic research, fearing that they will be exploited. "You don't want research subjects to feel cheated and embittered and betrayed," he said. "In the long run, for research with human subjects to survive, those human subjects have to feel that they've been treated fairly."

Originally published in the *New York Times Magazine*, May 15, 2006

You Be The Judge

Lesson 5

Your Money or My Life

Introduction

n the old Jack Benny routine, a robber holds up a man and says, “Your money or your life.” After a suitably dramatic pause, the man says, “Hold on a minute, I’m thinking, I’m thinking.”

There is no question that life is more valuable than money. Thus, one may steal or damage property in order to save a life. But is there any obligation to repay the owner for the loss incurred?

The Talmud offers some surprising answers to this question.

May One Steal or Damage Another's Property in Order to Save a Life?

Text 1

רבי יהודה ורבי יוסי הוו קא אזלי באורחא אחזיה בולמוס לרבי יהודה
קפחיה לרועה אכליה לריפתא

Rabbi Yehudah and Rabbi Yosi were walking together when a ravenous hunger seized Rabbi Yehudah. He seized a shepherd and devoured his meal.

Talmud, Yoma 83b

Text 2

"ויתאוה דוד ויאמר מי ישקני מים מבור בית לחם אשר בשער
ויבקעו שלשת הגבורים במחנה פלשתים
וישאבו מים מבור בית לחם אשר בשער"
רב הונא אמר: גדישים דשעורים דישראל הוו דהוו מטמרי פלשתים בהו
וקא מיבעיא ליה: מהו להציל עצמו בממון חבירו?
שלחו ליה: אסור להציל עצמו בממון חבירו
אבל אתה מלך פורץ לעשות לו דרך ואין מוחין בידו

David had a craving and said, "If only someone could give me water to drink from the well of Bethlehem, which is in the city gate!" So the three mighty men [of David] broke into the camp of the Philistines and drew water from the well of Bethlehem, which is at the gate . . . and they carried it and brought it to David (II Shmuel/Samuel 23:11-17).

Rav Huna said: "There were stacks of barley belonging to the Jews in which Philistines were hiding. [David wanted to set fire to the stacks to root out the enemy], so he asked [halachic guidance from the Sanhedrin], as follows: 'Is it permissible to save oneself through the destruction of someone else's property?' [The Sanhedrin] sent back to him [the following decision]: 'It is normally prohibited for a person to save himself through the destruction of someone else's property; but you, you are a king! [And a king] may break through fences [around another's property] to make a path for himself [and his armies] and no one may protest against him. [Thus you are permitted to burn the stacks of barley].'"

Talmud, Bava Kama 60b

Text 3

אסור להציל עצמו בממון חברו על דעת להפטר
אלא על דעת לשלם כשתמצא ידו הואיל ואפשר בתשלומין

It is prohibited to save oneself with someone else's money without intention to reimburse for the loss if one has the means to do so, as [there is no duress in not paying and] one has the choice to reimburse the owner [without subjecting oneself to danger].

Rabbi Shne'ur Zalman of Liadi, Shulchan Aruch HaRav, Laws of Theft, no. 2

Rabbi Shne'ur Zalman of Liadi (1745-1813), "the Alter Rebbe," author of *Tanya,* an early classic of Chasidism, *Torah Or, Likutei Torah,* and *Shulchan Aruch HaRav,* a halachic commentary. Rabbi Shne'ur Zalman founded the Chabad school of mysticism.

Limits of Liability for Theft and Damage Incurred in Saving a Life

Text 4

ונרדף ששיבר את הכלים ... של כל אדם חייב ...
ורודף שהיה רודף אחר רודף להציל ושבר כלים פטור
ולא מן הדין אלא שאם אי אתה אומר כן
אין לך אדם שמציל את חבירו מן הרודף

Someone who is running away from a killer and broke another person's vessels while running is liable for those vessels . . . Someone who is pursuing a pursuer in an attempt to save the life of the pursued and caused damage to the vessels of the pursuer of life, or anyone else's vessels, is exempt from repayment. This is not based on strict legal principle; rather, [it was legislated by the sages], for, if we would hold a savior of life liable for the damages he may cause, no one would want to save lives.

Talmud, Bava Kama 117b

Text 5

ספינה שחשבה להשבר מכובד המשוי
ועמד אחד מהם והקל מהמשא והשליך בים פטור
שהמשא שבה כמו רודף אחריהם להורגם
ומצוה רבה עשה שהשליך והושיעם
הגה: ויש אומרים דוקא שטעונה יותר מדאי דהוי המשוי כרודף
אבל אם אינה טעונה יותר מדאי ובא נחשול לטבען חייבים לשלם

If a ship is about to be capsized due to the overwhelming weight on the ship and one of the passengers throws some of the luggage overboard to save the ship, he is exempt from reimbursing the owner of the luggage, as we see the luggage as a "rodef" (a pursuer of life). The passenger who throws the luggage overboard does a great mitzvah since he saves lives . . . However, this is only true if someone overloaded the ship with his luggage. However, if the ship is not overloaded, but ominous waves of water are threatening to sink the ship during a storm, one who throws off some of the luggage in order to lighten the ship will be liable.

Rabbi Yosef Caro, Shulchan Aruch, Choshen Mishpat 380:4

Rabbi Yosef Caro of Safed (1488-1575), author of the *Shulchan Aruch,* "the Set Table," a compilation of Halachah recognized as authoritative by all Jewish communities. Born in Spain, he fled the Inquisition at the age of four with his family.

Learning Exercise

Let's review the principles that we have discussed by looking at some sample cases. You will find the principles you need to solve each case by referring back to Texts 4 and 5. In pairs, discuss how you would solve each case, and the principles on which you base each decision.

5A. Liability for Luggage Thrown Overboard in a Storm

Direct Cause of Danger	Liability for Casting off Luggage?
Last passenger(s) overload ship	
Waves, wind, storm	

Case Study One: The Case of the Burning Building

You are taking a walk and see smoke coming out of a building. A child is screaming from the second floor. You can't enter the house because the house is locked. So you break a window and manage to open the frontdoor and save the child's life.

You Be The Judge

Are you liable for the broken window?

Case Study Two: The Case of the Swerving Car

You are driving your car, when, to your horror, you realize you have lost your brakes. In a desperate attempt to avoid a fatal accident you instinctively turn off the road into someone's private property, slamming into the side of the house and causing substantial damage to the exterior wall.

You Be The Judge

1. Do you have to pay for the damage?

---

2. Is the case any different if you're trying to avoid hitting a child who ran in front of your moving vehicle, causing damage in the process?

Case Study Three: The Case of the Dropped Books

You are delivering, on behalf of a friend, a package of valuable books to someone. On the way, you notice a shady-looking character following you. He seems dangerous. So you start running. But the shady character is in better shape than you, especially since he has no load weighing on his back the way you do. In order to save your life, you decide to drop the load of books and run as fast as you can. You escape the danger and decide after a while to go back in order to recover the package of books. Unfortunately, they are gone.

You Be The Judge

1. Do you have to pay for the books?

2. Would the outcome be different if the shady character caught you and told you at gunpoint to hand over the books?

A True Case from the Holocaust Case Study Four: The Case of the Hidden Treasure

Text 6

During World War II, Benjamin and Herman Gross each hid a large sum of money in different places, to remain till after the war. When the Nazis captured Herman, he pointed out to the soldiers the area where Benjamin's money was hidden so that they would spare him [Herman]. After the war, Benjamin sued his brother Herman before the Rabbinical Supreme Court in Tel Aviv for the value of the treasure he had revealed. Benjamin argues that Herman should have used his own money in order to save his life. Herman does not deny the fact that he revealed his brother's hiding place, but claims that the SS men had already been told by an informer about Benjamin's money and that they asked him directly for the location of Benjamin's hiding place. There was no mention made of Herman's own money. Thus, his life depended upon revealing the location of Benjamin's money, and he should therefore be exempt from repayment.

Rabbi Yitzchak Frankel (former Chief Rabbi of Tel Aviv) in *Techumin* 1:303

You Be The Judge

Based on what we have learned so far, do you think Herman has an obligation to repay his brother Benjamin for his lost treasure?

Text 7

אנסו המלך למוסר זה עד שיראה לו ממון חבירו שהוא בורח מלפניו והראה לו מפני האונס
הרי זה פטור שאם לא יראה לו יכהו או ימיתיהו

If a ruthless ruler forces someone to reveal the belongings of a friend, that person is exempt from repaying the loss, because it was an act done under life-threatening circumstances.

Mishneh Torah, Laws of Damages, 8:1-4
(cited in Shulchan Aruch, Choshen Mishpat. 388:3)

Rabbi Moshe ben Maimon (1135-1204), better known as Maimonides or "Rambam," author of *Mishneh Torah,* a compendium of Jewish law, and *Guide to the Perplexed*. Maimonides was born in Cordoba, Spain. After the conquest of Cordoba by the Almohades, who sought to forcibly convert the Jews to Islam, Maimonides fled and eventually settled in Cairo. There he became the leader of the Jewish community and in later life served as court physician to the vizier of Egypt. Maimonides, known for his rational approach to faith, argued that there could be no real contradiction between truth revealed by God and the truths demonstrable by human reason.

Questions for Discussion

1. Does it make a difference whether the person who is pressured to reveal someone else's belongings (or money) has his own money? Would we say that in that case he should have appeased the ruler with his own money, rather than giving away someone else's money?

2. What would be the law if the ruler did not specify the other person's belongings or money, but merely coerced someone to give him some money and in response to this coercion one points to someone else's money?

The Legal and the Mystical

Text 8

mitzvah without a mental initiative cannot ascend above.

Zohar, vol. 3, p. 306

Text 9

prayer without mental concentration is like a body without a soul.

Rabbi Schne'ur Zalman of Liadi, Tanya, ch. 38

Key Points

1. One is permitted to violate any prohibition, with the exception of committing any of the three major transgressions, in order to save a life, including the prohibitions against theft and destruction of other people's property.

2. One is required to reimburse the owner of the property for the loss incurred in the process of saving a life—whether one's own or the life of another.

3. The Sages legislated a special exemption for those who cause damage in the process of saving another person, because they wanted to encourage passersby to intervene to preserve life in such circumstances.

4. One is not liable for repayment of financial loss when the object is a "rodef"—an object that actively threatens the life of the individual by its presence.

5. One is liable for repayment in the case of destruction of any object that simply blocks the escape from danger.

6. One who causes financial loss to others in response to the direct instruction of a ruthless ruler is not liable for the action, but one who chooses of his own volition to create such a loss in order to appease a ruthless ruler is not exempt.

Additional Readings

Stealing To Save Someone's Life

By Charles J. Harary, Esq.

Mr. Harary is associated with the law firm of Davis, Polk & Wardwell.

To what extent can a person go to save a life? Can he steal? Can he destroy the property of another? If so, what is he liable for? Must he compensate the owner of the property? Consider the following famous scenarios:

1. "A" is stranded in a remote area by an unexpected blizzard. He breaks into an unoccupied cabin and waits for three days until the storm abates and he may safely leave. During that time, the backpacker consumes the food stocks in the cabin and breaks up his unknown benefactor's furniture, burning it in the fireplace to keep warm.[1]

2. "H," a diabetic, loses his insulin in an automobile accident. Before "H" lapses into a coma, he rushes to the house of "C," another diabetic. "C" is not at home, but somehow "H" manages to get into her house. After first assuring himself that he has left "C" enough insulin for her own daily dosage, "H" takes the insulin he needs to survive.[2]

I. The Approach of Jewish Law

A. Saving one's own life

G-d, through the words of the Torah, places utmost importance on the value of life. In Vayikra, the verse states: "ushmartem et chukotay ve'et mishpatai asher ya'ase otam ha'adam, vechai bahem, ani hashem."3 You shall observe my decrees and my laws that each man shall carry out and by which he shall live, I am G-d. This verse teaches us that the commandments were not meant to take precedence over human life. If the observance or the performance of a Torah law would create a risk to a human life, then preservation of that life should take precedence over the observance of that Torah law.

The Gemara in Sanhedrin 4 rules on the basis of this verse that if someone is offered the ultimatum to violate one of the prohibitions in the Torah or be killed, that person has the duty to violate that law and save his life. This rule applies to all the prohibitions in the Torah with three exceptions. The three exceptions are the prohibitions of idol worship, illicit sexual relations and murder. Although the Torah specifically says "vechai bahem," if a person would be given the ultimatum to violate one of these three transgressions or be killed, he must refuse to violate the prohibition and sacrifice his own life.

The same Gemara in Sanhedrin,[5] describes a case where a person being pursued destroys the property of another in effort to save his own life. Rava rules that if the property belongs to the pursuer, then the pursued is exempt from compensating the damage. However, if the person being pursued destroys the property belonging to a third party, he is liable for the damage. We see from this Gemara that it is permissible to destroy another's property to save your own life, provided that you compensate the owner of the property.

It seems from the pasuk "vechai bahem" and from the Gemara in Sanhedrin that only the three major transgressions take precedence over saving one's life; all other laws may be violated for pikuach nefesh. Since stealing or destroying property is not one of the three exceptions to the rule of "vechai bahem," it would seem obvious that one should steal and destroy property rather than die. The Raavad in fact rules this way.[6]

Despite the seeming clarity, there are sources that indicate that one may not steal even if it is for pikuach nefesh. The Binyon Tzion, Rav Yaakov Ettlinger, brings two sources that show authorities of the opinion that it is forbidden for a person to steal even if his life depends on it.[7]

The first source is a Gemara in Bava Kamma[8] that relates a story from Sefer Shmuel about King David.[9] King David was fighting the Philistines when he became very thirsty. He said "if only someone could give me water to drink from the well of Bethlehem which is in the city of the gate." Upon hearing this, three of David's men broke through the gate and retrieved water. Before drinking, David sent a question to the Sanhedrin, asking permission to drink the water, to which they responded in the negative. The Gemara understands the passage to be speaking of David's wish for halachic guidance. The "mayim" being referred to was not physical water but the waters of torah. According to R' Huna, the question David was asking was whether he was permitted to destroy the property of another for pikuach nefesh. David and his army were in the middle of a barley field where the Philistines were hiding. He wanted to torch the field so that the Philistines would retreat and thereby avoid an ambush on his army. The problem was that the barley field belonged to another Jew. David inquired if he could save himself and his army by sacrificing the property of another. The Gemara states that the Sanhedrin sent him back a ruling that it was forbidden to destroy the property of another to save his life, however since he is king, he has the power to do what he wants with the property of his people.[10]

From this Gemara a conflict arises between Rashi and Tosafos. Tosafos maintains that David was not asking the Sanhedrin if property destruction was permitted to save a life, because that was obviously permitted. David was aware of the rule that when there is a possible danger to life, one may transgress any sin in order to escape the danger, with the exceptions of idolatry, forbidden relations and murder.[11] Thus, one is clearly allowed to destroy someone else's property in order to remove a threat to life. David's question was whether he was liable to compensate the owner if he burnt the field. The Sanhedrin responded that it was forbidden to burn the property without compensating the owner. Tosafos further explains that the reason this rule is stated in the gemara in terms of a prohibition (It is prohibited for a person to save himself...) is to imply a caveat where there is another way to save oneself that does not entail the destruction of another's property, one is indeed prohibited from destroying that property.[12]

The Rosh[13] agrees with Tosafos and states that the Gemara never contemplated whether it was forbidden to save the life of the Jewish army at the expense of someone else's crops. Such a ruling was obvious since nothing stands in the way of pikuach nefesh except the three cardinal sins. David was inquiring about compensation to which the Sanhedrin responded was obligatory.

The Binyon Tzion states that Rashi disagrees with Tosafos' understanding of the Gemara and maintains that the Gemara should be interpreted literally.14 King David asked whether he could burn the field to save his soldiers, which the Sanhedrin prohibited. According to Rashi, a person is not allowed to steal or damage another person's property even under threat of death and even if one will repay the loss. Therefore it is Rashi's opinion that one may not steal even if it is for pikuach nefesh.

The second source that the Binyon Tzion discusses is a Gemara in Kesubos,[15] that describes a scenario where a witness is given the ultimate to sign a false note, which will award money to an undeserving party, or be killed. Rav Chisda says that Rav Meir rules that in such a case one should allow himself to be killed rather than sign the note since signing the false note would be stealing. Rava disagrees with the view of Rav Chisda and rules that the witness may sign the note since nothing stands in the way of mortal danger other than the three cardinal sins, which stealing is not a part of. The Rambam states that Rav Chisda's interpretation of Rav Meir is correct, and brings a Braisa Kitzonis (excluded beraisa) to show that Rav Meir adds theft to the list of the cardinal sins holding that stealing is a form of killing. Additionally, the Shitta Mekubetzes in Kesubos[16] quotes from the Rambam that the question of whether or not stealing should be the fourth of the cardinal sins may be a matter of dispute among the Tanaim.

In addition, there are sources that seem to imply that stealing is forbidden even for pikuach nefesh. Meseches Yoma[17] records a story where a Tanna stole a loaf of bread from a farmer in order to save his life, and was rebuked for doing so. In Bava Kamma[18] there is a case where the Rabbis objected to a person keeping in his possession an animal that grazed other people's property, thereby stealing from others even though the animal was needed to save the owner's life. The Yershalmi in Avoda Zara[19] implies that stealing is equal to the three cardinal sins of Judaism. Forcing someone to steal is like forcing him to kill. Since one cannot kill to save a life, one cannot steal either. The Beraisa in Meseches Semachos[20] compares one who steals to one who murders and worships idols; the Vilna Goan[21] compares a thief to an adulterer and a violator of Shabbos. From these sources, we can see that although theft is not formally on the list of cardinal sins, there are authorities that believe that theft is similar enough to murder, adultery and idolatry that it is forbidden to transgress even at the expense for the sake of pikuach nefesh.

Despite these sources, the halacha follows the views that one can steal for pikuach nefesh, but only on the condition that the property be returned or the owner compensated for the property's value.[22] The Shulchan Aruch[23] states that, except for idolatry, illicit relations and murder, a person is permitted to transgress all the sins in the Torah rather than be killed. Therefore, if a person's life is in danger and he must steal to save himself, he can do so. However, he must have the specific intention to pay back the owner. The Rambam[24] rules that if a person commands a Jew to transgress one of the commandments or be killed, he should transgress rather than be killed. He learns this rule from the pasuk "vechai bahem." Moreover, if a person is in this situation and chooses to die, he is guilty on his life.[25] The Rambam applies the law to all commandments except idolatry, illicit relations and murder.[26]

In conclusion, the dominant view in Jewish law follows the Shulchan Aruch[27] and the Rambam, which allow a person to steal or damage property of another to save his own life. Thus, one may break in to the house of another, or steal insulin if that was necessary to save his life. However, such a person must compensate the owner of the property.[29]

B. Saving the life of another

Saving the life of another Jew takes precedence over any monetary interest. The Torah commands, "lo ta'amod al dam re'echa,"[30] "thou shall not stand idly by the blood of they neighbor." This verse obligates all Jews to be Good Samaritans by commanding them to rescue another Jew in distress. This obligation is so fundamental that a person must go to any extent necessary in order to save the life of a fellow Jew.[31] Refusing to do so is considered a transgression.[32] The mitzvah of saving another is so important, that the Rabbis enacted a law exempting the rescuer from punishment resulting from any tort committed in the course of the rescue. The basic law of torts in halacha is that man is always forewarned and hence liable for damages whether he acts inadvertently or willfully, under coercion or voluntarily.[33]

The exception is for a rescuer, for a rescuer is exempt from the damages he causes during his attempted rescue. According to the Rambam, if one chases after the pursuer in order to rescue the pursued, and he breaks objects belonging to the pursuer or to anyone else, he is exempt.[34] The Rambam explains that this rule does not conform with the usual biblical law but is a special enactment by the Rabbis in order to prevent people from refraining to save others or being too careful during their rescue for fear of having to compensate for any damages done. In Bava Kamma,[35] Rabba states that although this rule seems to be violating the usually strict tort law, one can justify this leniency for the public interest for if this rule would not exist, no one would put himself out to rescue another from the hands of the pursuer.

II. The Approach of US Law

Due to the unique aspect of this legal issue relating to whether one can steal or destroy property in order to save life, I included a broader view of different laws relating to this topic. This section will review (i) American case law; (ii) English case law; (iii) Admiralty law and (iv) the Restatements, in order to fully address this topic.

A. American Case Law

In discussing the justifiability of destroying property in order to save life, the starting point invariably is Vincent v. Lake Erie Transportation Co.,[36] a case decided by the Supreme Court of Minnesota in 1910. In Vincent, plaintiff owned a wharf in which ships docked to unload cargo. Defendants owned a steamship that docked at plaintiffs' wharf to unload.[37] During the unloading process a storm developed which, by the time the unloading process was completed, was producing winds of fifty miles per hour[38] The storm continued to increase in intensity throughout the night[39] After defendants discharged all the cargo, plaintiff signaled for a tug to be cut loose from the dock. However, due to the severity of the storm, no tug could be obtained.[40] In the course of keeping fast to the dock, the wind and waves struck the steamship with such force "that she was constantly being lifted and thrown against the dock, resulting in its damage, as found by the jury, to the amount of $500."[41] Plaintiffs sued for the damage to the dock, and the court found in their favor. In the opinion, the court stated that although defendants were justified in not attempting to leave the dock during the storm,[42] they were responsible to the dock owners to the extent of the injury inflicted.[43] The court stated in dicta,

"theologians hold that a starving man, without moral guilt, take what is necessary to sustain life; but it could hardly be said that the obligations would not be upon such a person to pay the value of the property so taken when he became able to do so. And so public necessity may require the taking of private property for public purposes; but under our system of jurisprudence compensation must be made."[44]

The dicta in Vincent supports the position that although the law allows a person to sacrifice the property of another to save his life, an issue not involved in Vincent,[45] he must compensate the owner for such property compensation,[46] even if one is not at fault in creating the life-threatening situation.[47]

Another major case dealing with this issue is Ploof v. Putnam.[48] Ploof was decided by the Supreme Court of Vermont only two years prior to Vincent. In Ploof, defendant was the owner of a dock attached to an island. Plaintiffs, a husband, wife and two minor children, were sailing on the lake when a storm arose, placing them in great danger.[49] Whereupon, "to save these from destruction or injury" plaintiffs were compelled to secure the boat to defendant's dock.[50] After plaintiff secured the boat, defendant sent his servant to release plaintiffs' boat that was driven upon the shore by the storm. As a result, plaintiffs' boat was destroyed and the plaintiffs sustained injuries."[51] Plaintiffs sued defendant for trespass (i.e., battery) and trespass on the case (i.e., negligence).[52] The court found for the plaintiff and held that a landowner cannot prevent someone from trespassing to save his life. The court places a duty on the landowner to fade away in such privileged and necessary conditions. The judge awarded plaintiff damages for losses suffered, and stated that a condition of that necessity justifies entries upon land and interferences with personal property that will otherwise be considered trespass.[53] The court reasoned by analogy that since the law allows trespass to save chattels, then surely trespass to save human life is permissible. The court ruled that one may trespass onto the property or sacrifice the personal property of another to save his life or the lives of his fellows.[54]

B. English Case Law

The primary case cited in Ploof was Mouse's Case,[55] an English case decided in King's Bench in 1609. In Mouse's Case, the personal property of the plaintiff had been thrown overboard by a fellow passenger to lighten a barge that was in danger of sinking.[56] The plaintiff subsequently brought an action in trespass against the passenger who had jettisoned his property.[57] The court non-suited the plaintiff and declared that, "for the safety of the lives of passengers . . . it is lawful for any passenger to cast the things out of the barge."[58] The court added that the owners would have a remedy against the ferryman for overloading if they had overloaded the barge. However if "the danger accrued only by the act of G-d, as by tempest, no default being in the ferryman, everyone ought to bear his loss for the safeguard and life of a man."[59]

C. Admiralty Law

The principle that property may be destroyed to save human life is recognized in United States admiralty law as well. In modern times, if the circumstances involved in Mouse's Case had arisen within the admiralty jurisdiction,60 all of the cargo and the vessel itself would have been assessed a general average contribution to pay for the portion of the cargo that was jettisoned, but no contribution would have been assessed against those whose lives were saved.61

In summary, the very few cases addressing the issue have unanimously held that property may be destroyed when necessary to save human life. These cases have also held that no compensation is payable for having done so, if the person who destroys the property was not at fault in creating the life-threatening danger which necessitated the destruction of property. Nevertheless, the dicta in Vincent that required such compensation has affected the Restatement of Torts.

D. The Restatements

There are a number of provisions in the Restatement of Torts, (1934)[62] and the Restatement Second of Torts (1965)[63] that seem to support the position that one may sacrifice personal property of another to save his own life but he must compensate the owners of the property afterward. In Section 197 of both the original Restatement and the Restatement Second, the Restatement takes the position that one is privileged to enter the land of another in order to prevent serious harm to the life, land or chattel of oneself or others.[64] A person who enters under this privilege, however, must pay compensation for any damages.[65]

In Section 263, the Restatement deals with trespass and conversion of chattels. The Restatement limits the privilege to situations in which chattels were destroyed or used to save life or to avoid serious bodily harm66 and takes no position as to whether one is authorized to take a chattel over the objection of its owner.[67] Section 263 of the Restatement (Second) not only extends the privilege to cover the destruction or use of chattels to save property, but also permits the taking of property even if its possessor objects.[68] The person destroying or using the property is, however, liable for any harm done.[69] The reason given by the drafters of both the Restatement and the Restatement (Second) for recognizing a "privilege" to destroy or use others' chattels to save one's property is the same; to take from the possessor of the chattel "the privilege ... to use reasonable force to defend his exclusive possession."[70] The Reporter's notes to the Restatement Second however admits that "there is scarcely any authority to support the principle stated in this Section, and it must rest largely upon the analogy to the corresponding privilege to interfere with the exclusive possession of land, stated in 197."[71] There then follows a "see" citation[72] to Mouse's Case that, as we have seen, held that no compensation is due when property is destroyed to save life.[73] The Restatements fail to cite any cases in which compensation was actually awarded when property was destroyed in order to save life.

A case decided subsequent to the publication of the Restatement Second, however, does offer some support for the position taken by the two Restatements. In Ruiz v. Forman,[74] a driver swerved to avoid an oncoming vehicle and entered the plaintiff's land, causing $270 worth of property damage.[75] The jury found for the defendant but the trial court granted the plaintiff's motion for judgment notwithstanding the verdict.[76] When the case reached the appellate court, the parties stipulated that the defendant had intentionally entered the plaintiff's land.[77] If that were so, the court declared, the case would clearly come within the ambit of section 197 of the Restatement (Second) as a privileged entry onto the property of another.[78] The "culpable or moral fault, if any, is said to be attributed to the actor's refusal to pay for the damage done in the course of serving his own interests rather than in what he did," while "the legal fault centers around the notion that there was an intentional invasion of a legally protected interest."[79] These considerations "would afford a basis for a simple affirmance of the case."[80] It is interesting that the only case that clearly echoes the Restatement Second, is one that cites the Restatement Second as its sole authority.

E. Conclusion

In conclusion, the issue is not whether a person can steal or destroy property to save his life or the life of others since it is accepted in American law that such an action is permissible. The issue is whether such a person must compensate the owner if he did not create the danger. There are few cases directly on point but the weight of such cases conflict with the position taken by sections 197 and 263 of the Restatements.[81] These cases and the doctrines of admiralty law support the contention that when neither the actor nor those whose lives are saved are legally at fault for placing themselves in the perilous position from which they can only be saved by destroying the property of another, they bear no legal liability for destroying that property.

F. Saving the life of another

American law, unlike Jewish law, takes a different approach in rescuing others. American law places no duty on a person to save another in danger. Even if one attempts to go beyond the letter of the law and tries to save another in distress, he can be liable for damages caused, even if the person suing is the person he attempted saving.[82] Since the law, however, generally permits a person to steal or destroy property to save oneself, it would be logical to assume the same would apply to saving others. On the issue of whether a rescuer would have to compensate the owner of the property. Francis Bohlen asserts that where others' lives, but not one's own, are at stake, property may be destroyed without any corresponding obligation to pay compensation.[83] Robert Keeton generally supports the position taken by the Restatements but is skeptical about whether a person who destroys property to save the lives of others has any obligation to pay for the property.[84]

III. Contrast Between American and Jewish Law

American law is similar to Jewish law regarding the issue whether a person can steal or destroy property to save lives. Although the law does seem similar, American law is not as definite as Jewish law. The cases that have created the American legal precedent were cases where the act was approved by society. Trespassing onto land to save yourself during a storm, throwing baggage overboard to save the lives of others are examples of scenarios that the courts have faced in creating such precedent. One wonders what the law would be if the cases that came before the same courts involved situations where society did not agree with the action. Would the law be so forgiving if it involved a homeless person stealing to eat, or a person infected with AIDS stealing medication to live? The precedent, although clear, is weak. Future cases will probably be decided on a case-by-case basis, and the law will depend on the discretion, and the compassion, of the presiding judge. In contrast, the Jewish law is far more definite. Since Jewish law stems from G-d, deciphered through the words of the Torah, less discretion is given to presiding authorities. Therefore to a larger extent the issue has been resolved and no matter what the case will be, the law will stay far more constant than American law.

Notes

1 See Joel Feinberg, Voluntary Euthanasia and the Inalienable Right to Life, 7 Phil. & Pub. Aff. 93, 102 (1978).

2 See Jules L. Coleman, Risks and Wrongs 282 (1992).

3 Vayikra 18:5.

4 Sanhedrin 74a.

5 Sanhedrin 74a.

6 Chapter 8 of Halachos Chovel Umezik Halacha 4.

7 See Responsa of the Binyon Tzion §167-§171.

8 Bava Kamma 60b.

9 There are two places where this incident is described in essentially the same language. See Shmuel B 23:11-17 and Divrie Hayamim A 11:13-19.

10 This relates to the modern day law of eminent domain.

11 See Sanhedrin 74a.

12 See also Yad Ramah to Sanhedrin 74a; Tur Choshen Mishpat §359.

13 Rosh to Sanhedrin 8:2.

14 See Binyon Tzion Responsa §166- §171.

15 19a.

16 D'H V'od.

17 Yoma 83b.

18 80a.

19 Chapter 2, Halacha 2.

20 Chapter 2, Halacha 11.

21 Noshchat HaGra 1.

22 Choshen Mishpat 359:4 and 380:3.

23 Choshen Mishpat 359:4.

24 Chapter 5, Hilchos Yesodei Hatorah, Halachos 1 and 2.

25 Chapter 5, Hilchos Yesodei Hatorah, Halachos at 1.

26 Chapter 5, Hilchos Yesodei Hatorah, Halachos at 2. The Rambam, however, limits the generalization to times when there are no evil decrees on the Jews. However when evil decrees are imposed on the Jews, a Jew must not transgress any commandments, but rather be killed.

27 Choshen Mishpat 380:3.

28 Rambam, Hilchos Chovel U'Mezik, Chapter 8:13.

29 It is interesting to note an additional conflict on this topic. If it is impossible for compensation to be made, the Binyon Tzion rules that even according to the majority opinions, stealing is prohibited. The Maharam Shick and the Shulchan Aruch disagree and state that although the halacha obligates the condition of reimbursement, if you are unable to pay back the owner, you still are able to steal for pikuach nefesh.

30 Vayikra 19:16.

31 Rashi, Sanhedrin 73a.

32 Rambam, Hilchos Rotzeach U'Shmiras Nefesh 1:14, summarizing the discussion in Sanhedrin 73a.

33 See Sanhedrin 72a; Rambam, Hilchos Chovel Umezik, 1:12; 6:1.

34 See Rambam, Chovel U'Meizik 8:12.

35 117b.

36 124 N.W. 221 (Minn. 1910).

37 Id.

38 Id.

39 Id.

40 Id.

41 Id.

42 Id.

43 Id at 222.

44 Id.

45 There is no indication in Vincent that the storm presented a danger to the lives of the crew.

46 See Jules L. Coleman, Risks and Wrongs, 300-01 (1992); See also Joel Feinberg, Voluntary Euthanasia and the Inalienable Right to Life, 7 Phil. & Pub. Aff. 93, 103 (1978).

47 See Jules L. Coleman, Risks and Wrongs, 292-96 (1992).

48 81 Vt. 471 (Vt. 1908).

49 Id at 473.

50 Id.

51 Id. at 474.

52 Id.

53 Id.

54 Id at 475.

55 77 England. Rep. 1341 (K.B. 1609), cited with approval in Ploof, 81 Vt. at 475.

56 See id. at 1341-42.

57 See id.

58 Id. at 1342.

59 Id at 1342; see also Ploof, 81 Vt. at 475 (citing Mouse's Case, 77 England. Rep. 1341, and quoting this passage).

60 See 28 U.S.C. 1333 (1994).

61 See Gustavus H. Robinson, Handbook of Admiralty Law in the United States 778-79 (1939) (describing the "general average" rule). Both the Convention for the Unification of Certain Rules with Respect to Assistance and Salvage at Sea, Sept. 23, 1910, 37 Stat. 1658, and its successor, the International Convention on Salvage, Apr. 28, 1989, Hein's No. KAV 3169 Provide that "no remuneration is due from the persons whose lives are saved," although both conventions also provide that "nothing in this article shall affect the provisions of the national law on this subject."

62 See Restatement of Torts 197 (1934).

63 See Restatement (Second) of Torts 197 (1965).

64 See Restatement 197(1); Restatement (Second), 197(1).

65 See Restatement (Second), 197(2). The first Restatement required the payment of compensation when a person destroyed property to protect his own interests, but took no position on whether one who acted to protect the interests of third party was obliged to pay compensation. See Restatement, 197(2) & 197 first caveat.

66 See Restatement of Torts 25, 263(1) (1934) ("One is privileged to use or otherwise intentionally intermeddle with a chattel while in the possession of another for the purpose of protecting himself, the other, or a third person from death or serious bodily harm ....").

67 See id.

68 See Restatement (Second), 263 cmt. b ("Since the actor does not become a trespasser when making reasonable use of or otherwise intermeddling with another's chattel to protect himself or another, such intermeddling

cannot be restricted by the possessor of the chattel.").

69 See id. 263(2) ("Where the act is for the benefit of the actor or a third person, he is subject to liability for any harm caused by the exercise of the privilege."). The first Restatement contained a caveat as to whether an actor was liable for damages to a chattel caused by his intermeddling for the benefit of a third party. See Restatement, 263 third caveat.

70 Restatement, supra note 62, 263 cmt. b; Restatement (Second), supra note 63, 263, cmt. b.

71 Restatement (Second) App., supra note 66, Reporter's notes to 263.

72 See id. The other case cited in the Reporter's notes to the Restatement (Second) is *McKeesport Sawmill Co. v. Pennsylvania Co.*, 122 F. 184 (W.D. Pa. 1903), which involved a runaway barge that became embedded in the defendant's bridge and which was destroyed in the process of dislodging it. The defendant was not required to compensate the plaintiff. See id at 187 (stating that the defendant does not have to try and save the plaintiff's property, but simply not to recklessly or unnecessarily injure or destroy it). It was clearly a type of self-defense.

73 See Mouse's Case, 77 Eng. Rep. 1341, 1342 (K.B. 1609).

74 514 S.W.2d 817 (Tex. Civ. App. 1974).

75 See id.

76 See id.

77 See id. at 818.

78 See id.

79 Id.

80 Id.

81 William L. Prosser, Handbook of the Law of Torts at 64-65 (4th ed. 1971).

82 See Prosser and Keeton, The Law of Torts at 375-378 (5th ed. 1984); See also J.R. Spencer, The Rescuer as Defendant, Cambridge Law Journal 28, 30-33 (1970).

83 See Francis H. Bohlen, Incomplete Privilege to Inflict Intentional Invasions of Interests of Property and Personality, 39 Harv. L. Rev. 307, 317-18 (1926).

84 See Robert E. Keeton, Conditional Fault in the Law of Torts, 72 Harv. L. Rev. 401, 415-18, 427-30 (1959).

You Be The Judge

Lesson 6
Burden of Proof

Introduction

You see two men go into a room with no windows and only a single entrance, and you hear the door lock behind them. After ten minutes, the door opens. One of the two men is lying face down on the ground, dead. You see human teeth marks on the back of his neck. There is only one possible explanation. The other man must have bitten him to death (since he could not have bitten himself on the back). Can the murderer be convicted on this evidence? Or, given that no one has directly witnessed the act, must he be allowed to go free?

Determining Truth
Biblical Roots

Text 1

לֹא יָקוּם עֵד אֶחָד בְּאִישׁ לְכָל עָוֹן וּלְכָל חַטָּאת בְּכָל חֵטְא אֲשֶׁר יֶחֱטָא
עַל פִּי שְׁנֵי עֵדִים אוֹ עַל פִּי שְׁלֹשָׁה עֵדִים יָקוּם דָּבָר

A single witness shall not stand up against any man for any iniquity or for any sin, regarding any sin that he may have committed. By the word of two witnesses or by the word of three witnesses shall a matter be confirmed.

Devarim/Deuteronomy 19:15

Two Witnesses

Text 2

שבכך נצטוינו כמו שנצטוינו לחתוך את הדין על פי שני עדים כשרים
ואף על פי שאפשר שהעידו בשקר
הואיל וכשרים הם אצלינו מעמידין אותן על כשרותן
ובדברים האלו וכיוצא בהן נאמר: "הנסתרות לה' אלהינו והנגלות לנו ולבנינו"
ונאמר: "כי האדם יראה לעינים וה' יראה ללבב"

We are commanded to issue a verdict on the basis of the testimony of two witnesses, even though there exists the possibility that they both are lying. Nevertheless, since they seem honest to us, we go by the general assumption that they are good people. It is about this issue that the Scripture tells us: The hidden things are for G-d [to deal with], but the revealed things are for us and for our children forever, to carry out all the words of this teaching (Devarim 29:28).

Maimonides, Mishneh Torah, Laws of the Foundations of the Torah 7:7

Rabbi Moshe ben Maimon (1135-1204), better known as Maimonides or "Rambam," author of *Mishneh Torah,* a compendium of Jewish law, and *Guide to the Perplexed*. Maimonides was born in Cordoba, Spain. After the conquest of Cordoba by the Almohades, who sought to forcibly convert the Jews to Islam, Maimonides fled and eventually settled in Cairo. There he became the leader of the Jewish community and in later life served as court physician to the vizier of Egypt. Maimonides, known for his rational approach to faith, argued that there could be no real contradiction between truth revealed by God and the truths demonstrable by human reason.

Text 3

The reason the law requires two witnesses for evidence in a court of law is not because we suspect a single witness of lying. Rather, it is a biblical axiom, which is true even if the witness is speaking the truth. Similarly, the law disqualifies witnesses who are related to each other, but not because of any possible biases involved, since even Moses and Aaron would be disqualified from testifying about the same incident.

Rabbi Aryeh Leib Heller, Ketzot Hachoshen 30:9

Rabbi Aryeh Leib Heller (1745-1813), author of *Ketzot Hachoshen,* a commentary on Halachah. He served for a time as rabbi in Rozniatow, Ukraine (Galicia).

Rational Evidence

Text 4

אמר רבי שמעון בן שטח:
אראה בנחמה אם לא ראיתי אחד שרץ אחר חבירו לחורבה
ורצתי אחריו וראיתי סייף בידו ודמו מטפטף והרוג מפרפר
ואמרתי לו: רשע מי הרגו לזה? או אני או אתה.
אבל מה אעשה שאין דמך מסור בידי
שהרי אמרה תורה "על פי שנים עדים יומת המת"
היודע מחשבות יפרע מאותו האיש שהרג את חבירו
אמרו: לא זזו משם עד שבא נחש והכישו ומת

Rabbi Shimon ben Shotach said: I once saw a man chase after his friend into a ruin. I ran after him [and when I entered the ruin]; I saw a sword dripping with blood in his hand, and his victim was lying dead [on the floor]. I told him: Evil one! Who killed this man? It is either you or me! But what can I do when your blood has not been delivered into my hands [for justice], as the Torah [explicitly] states: By the word of two witnesses or by the word of three witnesses shall the condemned person be put to death (Devarim 17:6). However, G-d will administer justice to you. It was told that the man, before leaving the ruin, was bitten by a snake and died.

Talmud, Sanhedrin 37b

Text 5

כי הדברים האפשריים מהם קרובי האפשרות מאד
ומהם רחוקי האפשרות ומהם אמצעיים בין זה לזה
ואילו התירה התורה לחתוך דיני נפשות
באפשר הקרוב מאד ולאפשר רוחב גדול מאד
שאפשר שיהיה קרוב מן המחוייב המציאות
כגון זה שהמשלנו היינו חותכים הגדר
במה שהוא רחוק מזה מעט ובמה שהוא יותר רחוק גם כן
עד שיחתכו הגדרים וימיתו האנשים פעמים במעט אומד
לפי דמיון הדיין ומחשבתו

Evidence that is based on probability has a margin of error. In some cases the margin of error is wider than in other cases. If the Torah had permitted the courts to punish in a case where the evidence is based on even the highest degree of probability, this would have led to punishing suspected criminals even when there was a slightly lesser degree of probability. Ultimately the courts would have begun to punish on the basis of evidence that is subjective to the intuition of the judge . . . in which case we might have ended up killing an innocent person.

Maimonides, Sefer Hamitzvot, Negative Commandment no. 290

Text 6

שור שהיה רועה על גב הנהר ונמצא שור הרוג בצדו
אף על פי שזה מנוגח וזה מועד ליגח, זה מנושך וזה מועד לישך
אין אומרין בידוע שזה נשכו וזה נגחו
אפילו גמל האוחר בין הגמלים ונמצא גמל הרוג בצדו
אין אומרין בידוע שזה הרגו עד שיראוהו עדים כשרים

If an ox was pasturing near a river and another ox was found killed (gored) right next to it, even if the pasturing ox had a history of aggressive behavior, such as goring other animals, we cannot assume that the aggressive ox gored the other one to death unless we have witnesses who observed the incident.

Maimonides, Mishneh Torah, Laws of Damages 8:14

Text 7

הרי שהלך בנו למדינת הים ושמע שמת בנו
ועמד וכתב כל נכסיו לאחר ואחר כך בא בנו
. . . אין מתנתו מתנה שאלמלי היה יודע שבנו קיים לא היה כותבן

A man heard that his son who had traveled abroad had just died. The father then gave all the son's property to a friend as a gift. Later on, the son returned home ... the gift is cancelled, for had he known that his son was alive, he would not have given all the property away to the friend.

Talmud, Bava Batra 146b

Applications
Case Study: Lost at Sea

Text 8

Two Jewish men embarked on a ship, owned and operated by an Arab company. The ship was heading for Algiers. As the ship approached its destination, the passengers were terrified by the sight of an approaching pirate ship from Italy. In order to escape, all the passengers jumped into the sea and began to swim to the shore. One of the Jewish passengers realized soon after jumping into the water that he would not be able to make it to the shore, so he went back to the ship. A miracle occurred when a sudden strong wind pushed the ship onto the shore before the pirates were able to attack it. The other Jew was nowhere to be found. The surviving Jew claimed that he saw his friend struggling in the waters. He didn't seem to know how to swim. Furthermore, upon reaching the shore, the surviving Jewish passenger claimed to have looked back at the sea and seen the body of his friend floating facedown lifelessly on the waters without any sign of life. There were also other statements heard from Arab passengers that claimed that the missing Jew was not taken hostage by the pirates, and that he definitely died in the wild waters of the sea.

The missing passenger has a son, the legal heir to his father's estate, who wishes to take control of

Rabbi Shimon bar Tzemach (1361-1444), known as "Tashbetz," born in Majorca. Because of forced conversions and massacres of Jews in Spain, he fled to Algiers in 1391, where he was able to resume his role as a rabbi. Known for his responsa, which address all aspects of Jewish life.

his father's estate. Can we assume that the father is indeed dead and that the estate has been legally transferred to the son's ownership?

Rabbi Shimon bar Tzemach, She'eilot Uteshuvot Tashbetz, vol.1, no. 74

Text 9

מי שהוחזקה אשת איש והלכה היא ובעלה למדינת הים
ושלום בינו לבינה ושלום בעולם
ובאה ואמרה מת בעלי נאמנת ותנשא או תתיבם
חזקה שאינה מקלקלת עצמה ותאסור עצמה על זה ועל זה
ותפסיד כתובתה מזה ומזה
ותוציא בניה ממזרים בדבר העשוי להגלות לכל
ואי אפשר להכחיש ולא לטעון טענה
שאם הוא חי סופו לבא או יודע שהוא חי
וכן אם בא עד אחד והעיד לה שמת בעלה
תנשא על פיו שהדבר עשוי להגלות
אפילו עבד או אשה או שפחה ועד מפי עד
מפי עבד מפי שפחה מפי קרובין
נאמנין לומר מת פלוני ותנשא אשתו או תתיבם על פיהם

A married woman who traveled with her husband overseas at a time when their relationship was peaceful, and peace abides in the world at large. If she comes and says, "My husband died," her word is accepted and she is granted permission to marry . . .

The rationale is: a woman will not bring difficulties upon herself, causing herself to be forbidden to both her first and her second husbands, causing herself to lose the right to collect the money due her by virtue of her ketubah from both husbands and causing her children to be deemed illegitimate when the matter is likely to become openly revealed, and when she will not be able to deny the matter or offer any argument in her defense. For if her husband is alive, he will ultimately return, or [at least, it will become known that he is alive].

Similarly, if one witness comes and testifies that the woman's husband died, she is granted permission to marry by virtue of his testimony, because the truth of the matter will ultimately be revealed. Similarly . . . a witness testifying on the basis of statements he heard from others is accepted regarding a person's death. On the basis of such testimony, the man's wife is granted permission to remarry . . .

Maimonides, Mishneh Torah, Laws of Divorce 12:15

Text 10

אל יקשה בעיניך שהתירו חכמים הערוה החמורה בעדות אשה . . .
ועד מפי עד ומפי הכתב ובלא דרישה וחקירה כמו שבארנו
לא הקפידה תורה על העדת שני עדים ושאר משפטי
העדות אלא בדבר שאין אתה יכול לעמוד על בריו
אלא מפי העדים ובעדותן
כגון שהעידו שזה הרג את זה או הלוה את זה
אבל דבר שאפשר לעמוד על בריו שלא מפי העד הזה
ואין העד יכול להשמט אם אין הדבר אמת
כגון זה שהעיד שמת פלוני לא הקפידה תורה עליו
שדבר רחוק הוא שיעיד בו העד בשקר

לפיכך הקלו חכמים בדבר זה והאמינו בו עד אחד
ובלא דרישה וחקירהכדי שלא ישארו בנות ישראל עגונות . . .

Do not wonder at the fact that our Sages discharged the prohibition against a married woman, which is considered a very severe matter, on the basis . . . of a written testimony or testimony that was not investigated by the ordinary process of interrogation, as we have explained.

These leniencies were instituted because the Torah requires testimony of two witnesses and all the other details of the laws of witnesses only with regard to matters that cannot be verified definitively except via witnesses and their testimony —e.g., that one person killed another, or that one person lent money to another. When, by contrast, the matter may be verified definitively without the testimony of a witness, and the witness cannot justify his statements if they are not true—e.g., when one testifies that a person died, they did not make necessary that a requirement of formal testimony be met in these instances. For it is unlikely that a witness will testify falsely.

For this reason, our Sages extended the leniency with regard to this matter and accepted the testimony of a single witness . . . The leniencies were accepted so that the daughters of Israel would not be forced to remain unmarried.

Maimonides, Mishneh Torah, Laws of Divorce 13:29

The Legal and the Mystical

Text 11

The role of testimony in a Jewish court of law is not only to logically establish the truth of a matter. The testimony of two valid witnesses is a divinely mandated requirement of the judicial process and a critical part of legal procedure. Without it, the rendering of judgment is incomplete.

Rabbi Menachem Mendel Schneerson (The Lubavitcher Rebbe)
Likutei Sichot, vol. 21, p. 62

Rabbi Menachem Mendel Schneerson (1902-1994), also known simply as "the Rebbe." Born in southern Ukraine. Rabbi Schneerson escaped from the Nazis, arriving in the U.S. in June 1941. The Rebbe emphasized the importance of traditional Jewish teachings concerning Mashiach, often reminding people that the performance of just one additional good deed could usher in the era of Mashiach.

Text 12

אַתֶּם עֵדַי נְאֻם ה' וְעַבְדִּי אֲשֶׁר בָּחָרְתִּי לְמַעַן תֵּדְעוּ וְתַאֲמִינוּ לִי וְתָבִינוּ כִּי אֲנִי הוּא

You are My witnesses [the word of G-d] and My servant that I have chosen so that they will know and believe Me and understand that I am He.

Yeshayahu/Isaiah 43:10.

Key Points

1. Courts may reach a decision either on the testimony of two witnesses or as a consequence of a logically compelling analysis.

2. Circumstantial or probabilistic evidence is not considered compelling.

3. Jewish law does find compelling the argument that people will not perjure if their lie might be discovered (thus destroying their credibility).

4. In the classical case, an *agunah* is a woman who is "bound" and unable to remarry because it is unproven whether her husband is dead.

5. Rabbis debate whether an *agunah* may be freed by a single witness because of rabbinic leniency or because a reasonable person would not lie in this case.

6. Two witnesses are believed, not because they are in principle infallible sources of information, but because the Torah establishes them as the means through which divine justice is revealed.

7. The Jewish people have the spiritual role of "witnesses" through which the divine is revealed in the physical world.

Additional Readings

Two Witnesses

By Yanki Tauber

By two witnesses . . . shall a thing be established.

Deuteronomy 19:15

Torah law distinguishes between two types of witnesses. The first type of witnesses ("witnesses," according to Torah, are never less than two individuals) "establish a thing" only in the sense that they inform us of its existence. For example, if Reuven borrows $100 from Shimon, the obligation for him to return the money exists regardless of whether there were witnesses to the loan or not. It is only that, without the witnesses, the court would not have sufficient proof of the existence of the obligation (should Reuven deny it) and could not compel Reuven to carry it out. This category of witnesses are called eidei birur—"clarifying witnesses."

A second category of witnesses literally "establish a thing": without their witnessing, the thing would not exist. For example, Torah law requires that a marriage be witnessed by two witnesses. Without these witnesses, the marriage does not take effect, even if all parties involved admit that everything else was in order. This category of witnesses are called eidei kiyum—"establishing witnesses"—for their witnessing of the event is an integral part of the process which establishes a new legal state.

The clarifying witness and the establishing witness are both "witnesses" in that they observe a certain fact or occurrence. But they differ greatly in their function and the manner in which they carry it out. Clarifying witnesses fulfill their function by testifying before the court—if they witness the loan but do not tell the court what they saw, their observation is of no legal significance. Establishing witnesses fulfill their function by observing the event—it is their observation itself that establishes the fact, even if they never testify to what they saw.

This essential difference between the clarifying witness and the establishing witness translates into various legal differences. For example, while Torah law requires that witnesses be cross-examined, this requirement applies only to clarifying witnesses, not to establishing witnesses.

Cross-examination is part of the testifying process: testimony can be properly understood and fully convincing to the court only when the witnesses are cross-examined. Thus, clarifying witnesses, whose function is to testify to the truth of an event or fact, require cross-examination. Not so establishing witnesses, whose witnessing of the event, rather than their testimony, is what establishes its truth.

Nature and Man

The Torah is G-d's blueprint for creation. When the Torah recounts an event that occurred at a particular point in history, or decrees a law regarding a particular conflict or relationship between two individuals, it is also describing the very structure of life and reality. Every story contains a universal truth; every law relates to our relationship with G-d and the purpose of our creation. The two different types of witnesses described above, and the legal distinctions between them, relate not only to the witnessing of loans and marriages, but also to the cosmic witnesses that establish the truth of all truths: the all-pervading truth of G-d.

Two types of witnesses attest to the divine reality: nature and man. "I set as witnesses before you today the heavens and the earth," says Moses to the children of Israel. For does not the earth, from the vital energy in its every blade of grass to the intricate structure of its every grain of dust, bespeak the wisdom of G-d? Does not the vastness of the heavens reflect the infinity of their Creator? "When I see Your heavens," sings King David, "the work of Your fingers, the moon and stars which You have ordained . . . the beasts of field, the birds of heaven, the fish of sea . . . O G-d our L-rd, how majestic is Your name in all the earth!"

The second witness is man. In the words of the prophet, "You are My witnesses, says G-d." Man bears witness to the truth of G-d through his observance of the mitzvot, the divine commandments. When a person puts on tefillin, the leather, parchment and ink out of which they are fashioned, the arm and head about which they are wrapped, the mind that meditates upon their significance and the heart that is aroused by the deed—these all become instruments of the divine will, the means by which a divine commandment is fulfilled. When a person contributes to charity, the hand that does the giving, the metal or paper that facilitates the exchange, and the energy and resources that were expended to earn the money, all become vehicles of G-dliness. In the words of the Midrash, the performer of a mitzvah is making "a dwelling for G-d in the physical world"—transforming the materials of his or her life into something that houses and realizes the divine truth.

Making Him Real

Both nature and the mitzvah-performing person are witnesses to the truth of G-d. Yet they differ greatly in the manner and function of their witnessing. The first is a "clarifying witness" who testifies to the divine essence of reality; the second is an "establishing witness" who makes real the divine in our world.

The heavens and the earth do not make G-d real—they only bespeak His reality. In fact, they only do so when "cross-examined in court"—when their testimony is coaxed from them by the astronomer's telescope and the psalmist's soul. In and of itself, the natural world actually conceals the divine presence; it is only through our examination and interrogation of nature that we make it speak and tell us about G-d.

Man on the other hand, is an "establishing witness": his life generates G-dliness. Our every performance of a mitzvah makes G-d a reality in this world, regardless of the extent to which we publicize our deeds or are even aware of what they achieve. Like the establishing witness, we effect an essential change in the reality to which we relate, regardless of whether we testify to what we have "witnessed."

Based on the Lubavitcher Rebbe's talks on various occasions.

Acknowledgments

MORE THAN TEN YEARS AGO, I approached **Professor Jeremy Rabkin** about my interest in teaching Talmud at Cornell University. Professor Rabkin responded enthusiastically, and together, we taught a well-received course in the government department comparing American and Talmudic law. It was Jeremy who initially proposed that we adopt the case method, an approach common in law school. That decision dynamically transformed the course. I am likewise grateful to Jeremy for countless insights that have done much to develop my thinking on this subject. The course that we taught together is the nucleus of the present one.

A number of the subjects discussed in the course became the basis for a series of articles I wrote for *Wellsprings Magazine.* **Mrs. Baila Olidort** helped prepare this material for publication, and two of the articles from the series are reprinted as additional readings in the student book.

The editorial board shaped the presentation of the course by providing thoughtful and detailed feedback. Thanks are due **Rabbi Ruvi New, Rabbi Nochum Schapiro,** and **Rabbi Yisrael Rice** for their comments. Special thanks to **Rabbi Hesh Epstein** and **Rabbi Averemel Sternberg** who offered extra guidance for the later lessons, often on very short notice. **Rabbi Berel Bell's** probing questions sharpened the focus of the lessons, and his suggested learning activities did much to clarify the central points.

The work of the production team is only apparent when it is faulty. It is a tribute to **Rhoda Rabkin,** our copyeditor, that you will not notice her work, but having responded to her numerous queries, I have new respect for the magnitude of her task.

Nachman Levine, who designed and laid out the text, brings to the work not only an artistic eye but a scholarly one, and is a fountain of useful information on topics as diverse as Talmudic references and the spelling of obscure place names. He has enriched this work in more ways than one. Thanks also to **Shimon Leib Jacobs,** who prints and distributes our books and brochures.

Special thanks to **chabad.org,** an invaluable online resource of Jewish learning and information, for providing many of the articles for our additional readings. **Meaningfullife.com** and **jlaw.com** have also graciously given permission for the reprinting of articles in our student books.

It has been a great responsibility and privilege to author this course for the **Jewish Learning Institute.** The undertaking of a project so ambitious has been made possible through the unwavering encouragement and support of our principal patron, vice chairman of Merkos L'Inyonei Chinuch-Lubavitch World Headquarters **Rabbi Moshe Kotlarsky,** and our principal benefactor, **Mr. George Rohr.** I thank **JLI**'s director, **Rabbi Efraim Mintz**, for his guidance and leadership, as well as the hard-working support staff at **JLI** Central, **Rabbi Yoni Katz, Rabbi Mendel Bell, Mrs. Rachel Druk,** and **Mrs. Nechama Shmotkin.**

As we enter the new year, it is my fervent wish that the **Jewish Learning Institute** continue to flourish, bringing the sweetness of Torah and the love of learning to communities around the world. I am grateful to HaShem for this opportunity to contribute in in some way to this growth.

Rabbi Eli Silberstein
Ithaca, New York
Ellul 5766

The Jewish Learning Multiplex

Brought to you by the Rohr Jewish Learning Institute

In fulfillment of the mandate of the Lubavitcher Rebbe, of blessed memory, whose leadership guides every step of our work, the mission of the Rohr Jewish Learning Institute is to transform Jewish life and the greater community through the study of Torah, connecting each Jew to our shared heritage of Jewish learning.

While our flagship program remains the cornerstone of our organization, JLI is proud to feature additional divisions catering to specific populations, in order to meet a wide array of educational needs.

The Rohr **JEWISH LEARNING INSTITUTE**

a subsidiary of Merkos L'Inyonei Chinuch,
the adult educational arm of the Chabad-Lubavitch movement

Torah Studies provides a rich and nuanced encounter with the weekly Torah reading.

MyShiur courses are designed to assist students in developing the skills needed to study Talmud independently.

This rigorous fellowship program invites select college students to explore the fundamentals of Judaism.

Jewish teens forge their identity as they engage in Torah study, social interaction, and serious fun.

The Rosh Chodesh Society gathers Jewish women together once a month for intensive textual study.

TorahCafe.com provides an exclusive selection of top-rated Jewish educational videos.

This yearly event rejuvenates mind, body, and spirit with a powerful synthesis of Jewish learning and community.

Participants delve into our nation's past while exploring the Holy Land's relevance and meaning today.

Select affiliates are invited to partner with peers and noted professionals, as leaders of innovation and excellence.

Machon Shmuel is an institute providing Torah research in the service of educators worldwide.

Made in the USA
Middletown, DE
01 November 2023